VIETNAM! VIETNAM!

VIETNAM! VIETNAM!

IN PHOTOGRAPHS AND TEXT

by FELIX GREENE

FULTON PUBLISHING COMPANY · PALO ALTO · CALIFORNIA

the case against

THIS BOOK IS ADDRESSED TO THE AMERICAN PEOPLE among whom I have been living for many years.

The war in Vietnam hangs over us all like a dark cloud. War, by its very nature is a cruel business. This war, however, differs from all others in which the United States has been engaged. In no previous conflict has this country deployed so fearful a concentration of power against so small a nation. In the sheer mechanical brutality with which it is being waged it is unique. Never before has the young manhood of America been thrust into such a conflict or ordered to fight with methods that outrage both the formal provisions of international law and the more general laws of our common humanity.

The case, such as it is, in support of the policies being pursued in Vietnam is propounded daily by members of the Administration, and their statements and speeches receive the widest possible publicity. This book presents the case against these policies. It does not pretend to be a full documentation, for that would require volumes. It does, however, set out in accurate sequence the salient events and decisions which, step by step, have led the richest and most powerful nation in the world to be drawn into a war with a very small and backward Asian nation.

Though it condemns without qualification the policies pursued by the political and military leaders of the U.S. in Vietnam, this book is not written in any spirit of malice, but rather with an unshakable faith in the essential generosity of the American people. I am wholly certain—and Secretary General U Thant has expressed much the same thought—that if the people of the United States only knew the background of the war in Vietnam, and what is being done there in their name, that they would insist on the war at once being brought to an end.

Thus, with admiration and respect, I dedicate this book to all Americans, in high places and in low, who by their actions and voices are opposing this war in Vietnam. One day it will be generally recognized that they are, by their opposition, affirming for all the world to see what is best and most humane in the American tradition.

Felix Greene

Published by the Fulton Publishing Company
Box 191, Palo Alto, California
Library of Congress Catalog Number 66-28359

Printed in the United States of America

contents

PHOTOGRAPHIC REPORT

THE UNITED STATES AND THE WAR IN VIETNAM

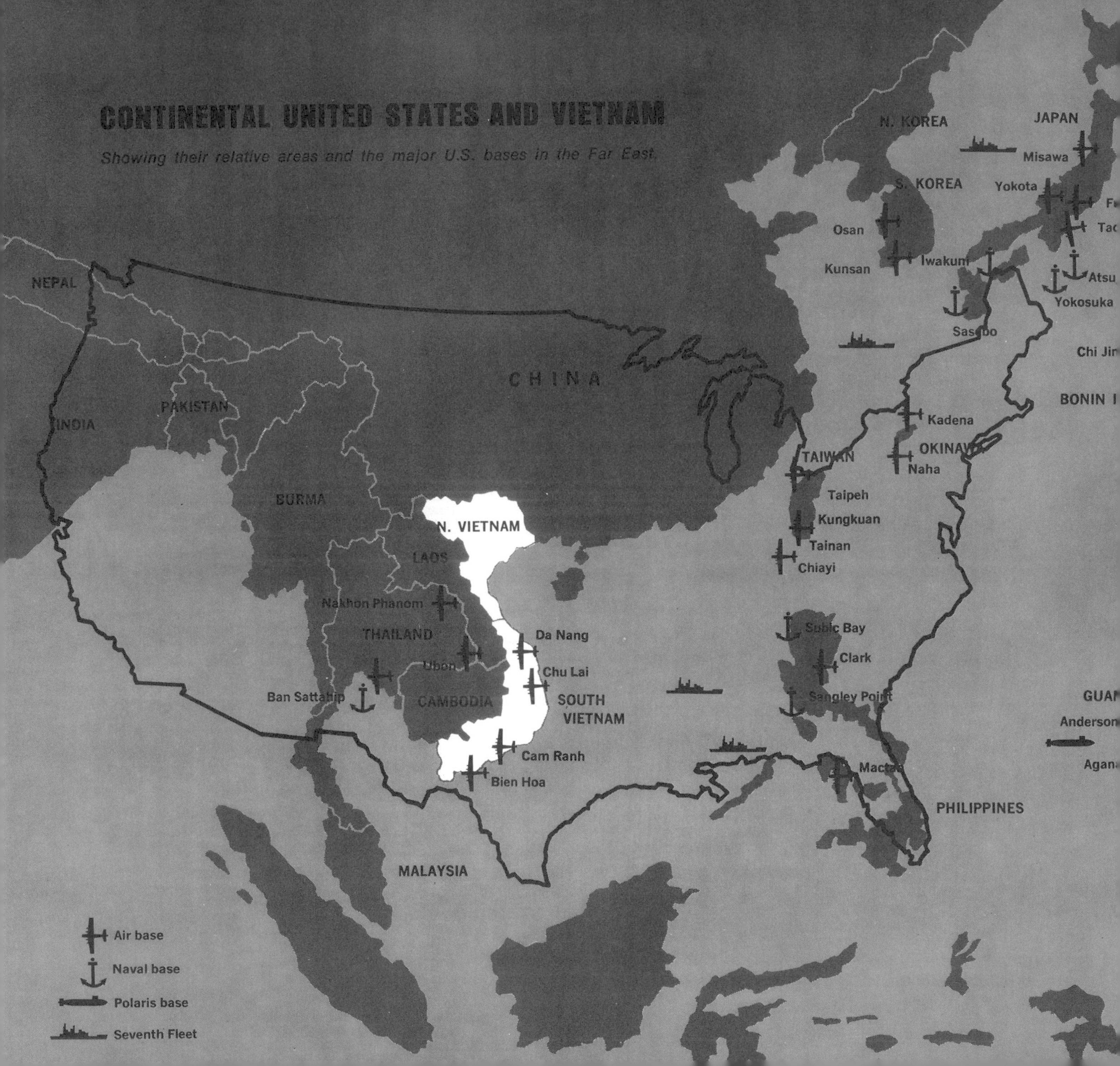
CONTINENTAL UNITED STATES AND VIETNAM
Showing their relative areas and the major U.S. bases in the Far East.
N. KOREA
JAPAN
Misawa
S. KOREA
Yokota
Osan
Kunsan
Iwakuni
Yokosuka
NEPAL
CHINA
PAKISTAN
INDIA
Kadena
OKINAWA
Naha
TAIWAN
Taipeh
Kungkuan
Tainan
Chiayi
BURMA
N. VIETNAM
LAOS
Nakhon Phanom
THAILAND
Ubon
Da Nang
Chu Lai
SOUTH VIETNAM
Ban Sattahip
CAMBODIA
Cam Ranh
Bien Hoa
Subic Bay
Clark
Sangley Point
PHILIPPINES
MALAYSIA
Air base
Naval base
Polaris base
Seventh Fleet

the land and its people

Vietnam is a small country and—by Western standards—a very poor one. In area it is one-twenty-eighth the size of the United States; in population, one sixth. The average Vietnamese earns in one year what the average American earns in a single week. He can expect to live only till he is thirty-five years old; an American can expect to live to seventy. This tiny country lies nine thousand miles away from Washington—and a hundred, or a thousand, years away in technology.

Within Vietnam, and as a living part of Vietnamese culture, are Buddhists, Catholics, Chinese, primitive mountain tribesmen, Cambodians, Thais. The Chinese ruled Vietnam for a thousand years, the French for eighty.

In spite of its small size and the poverty of its people, the Vietnamese look back with pride on a cultural history that goes back to before the time of Christ. Foreign domination and repeated invasions have given the Vietnamese a passion for independence and freedom from foreign control. The very variety of its population has bred in the Vietnamese an urgent need for national identity. Their history has shown that they are ready to endure almost unbelievable hardships to preserve it.

Physically, the Vietnamese are among the world's most beautiful people and, when allowed to live in peace, among the gentlest.

The autumn rice harvest is brought in by boat.

Nine out of ten Vietnamese are peasants living on the land. They are an industrious and amazingly hardy people.

As in most peasant countries, women take part in the work in the fields.

There is little motorized transport in the country-side. Much hauling is done by converted bicycles.

Threshing the rice crop.

Agricultural methods are simple—they have been handed down from generation to generation with little change. The peasants work hard. They live in harmony with the rhythm of the seasons, close to the soil that has nourished their people for over twenty centuries.

Processing fish sauce, a village industry in Thai Binh Province.

the West moves in

Vietnam, as so many other countries in Asia, felt the disruptive effects of the European industrial revolution. In the 19th Century, the growing industries of France demanded both raw materials and markets. The French colonies in Asia provided both.

In 1858 French troops invaded southeast Asia. By 1884 Indochina (comprising the countries we now know as Vietnam, Laos and Cambodia) was under French control.

The French system was devised to produce the maximum benefit to the French economy regardless of the destructive effect on the local population. Under the French, Indochina became the third largest exporter of rice and rubber in the world, but the people were poorer than they were before, and their own cultural patterns were deeply damaged.

Throughout the period of the French occupation there were constant peasant uprisings against the oppressive colonial rule. They were ruthlessly suppressed.

After sixty years of colonial government, the French were operating 81 prisons; only two per cent of the children were receiving elementary education; in all of Laos only one doctor had been trained. In 1943 the French spent five times more for the purchase of opium (to be sold by the government at a huge profit) than for the total combined expenditures on education, libraries and hospitals.

Such was the legacy of French colonialism in Vietnam.

he main street of Hanoi when
der the French.

In 1940 the Japanese invaded Vietnam. On orders from the Vichy Government the French in Vietnam offered no resistance, and for the first years of the war the French administered the colony for the Japanese.

The Japanese commander taking the French salute.

n 1945, a few months before their defeat, the Japanese ppointed a wealthy Vietnamese aristocrat, Bao Dai as a uppet "emperor" and through him took over the admin-stration of the country. Bao Dai was hated by his own peo-le. After the Japanese defeat, the Vietnamese declared heir independence and Bao Dai resigned.

ao Dai with U.S. Admiral Russell Berkey.

After World War II the French—with U.S. help—attempted to regain control of their former colony. French troops again invaded Vietnam. The French re-appointed Bao Dai as head of state.

French troops bringing in Vietnamese liberation fighters.

Ho Chi Minh, leader of the resistance against the French colonial government, and against the Japanese, symbolized the national determination to end all foreign domination.

The re-imposition of French colonial rule was intolerable to the Vietnamese and they took up arms to protect their newly independent Republic.

As the U.S. was to learn ten years later, to fight a people determined to be free of foreign domination is difficult.

"Those who refuse to learn from history", said George Santayana, "are doomed to repeat it."

Then as now . . . suspected guerrillas were brought in for questioning.

French troops embarking for the Far East. By 1954 there were 250,000 Frenchmen fighting in Vietnam.

80 per cent of the cost of the French war, and most of the equipment, was provided by the United States.

Then as now . . . French generals explained why success was certain.

Then as now . . . foreign mercenaries were sent to Vietnam to help fight the Vietnamese.

General de Castries, commander of the French forces at Dien Bien Phu.

Dien Bien Phu

In March 1954 the French hoped to bring the Vietnamese liberation forces into the open for a decisive battle at Dien Bien Phu. Instead, they were themselves trapped and surrounded. All supplies had to be parachuted in.

The defeated French troops after Dien Bien Phu

On May 7, after eight weeks of bitter fighting, the French garrison surrendered. With this defeat, French military influence in Southeast Asia came to an end.

In May 1954, a conference was called in Geneva to settle the political problems resulting from the end of French rule in Indochina.

The last session of the Geneva Conference.

the Geneva Conference

ANTHONY EDEN, *Britain*

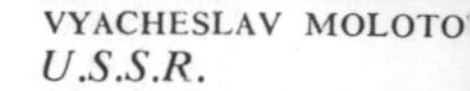

VYACHESLAV MOLOTO
U.S.S.R.

CHOU EN-LAI, *China*

GEORGES BIDAULT, *Fra*

PHAM VAN DONG,
Democratic Republic of Vietnam

JOHN FOSTER DULLES
U.S.A.

Nine nations participated in the Conference. The U.S. delegation made it clear that it was opposed to any settlement that would give independence to a united Vietnam.

Agreement was reached that Vietnam should be separated, for a temporary period only, into two zones; that elections under international supervision should be held not later than 1956; and that no participating powers would bring troops into either zone pending the elections. The U.S. did not agree to these conditions but promised it would not disturb them by force.

Diem inspecting his guard of honor.

ulles and Diem before a portrait of Washington.

the U.S. chooses Diem

Ngo Dinh Diem, a Vietnamese aristocrat and a former administrator under the French, had come to live in the United States. He received the support of important Catholics and others for his anti-Communist, anti-French policies. Without reference to the Vietnamese people, Diem was chosen by Secretary of State Dulles to be head of the Vietnamese Government.

By selecting Diem, the United States linked its authority, its treasure and its honor to the whims and dictates of a tyrant.

From this moment the U.S. was, step by step, drawn into an ever widening morass.

In the United States Diem continued to have the support of many influential people. The New York *Times* considered him "a man of deep religious heart". Lyndon B. Johnson called him "The Churchill of Vietnam".

Cardinal Spellman,
Archbishop of New York,
and President Diem.

Madame Nhu, Diem's sister-in-law, the first lady of Vietnam.

Diem's powerful and aristocratic family were totally out of touch with the aspirations and needs of the people of Vietnam who were living in ever-increasing destitution.

A Buddhist monk immolating himself in protest against the cruelties of Diem's regime. Buddhist opposition helped to bring down the Diem government.

Diem

No photographs could convey the dark tyranny of Diem's rule or the widespread misery to which it reduced his people.

The U.S.-Diem government failed to institute even the most urgently needed social reforms. The corruption and inefficiency of the small ruling elite brought the country to the brink of disintegration. There were periods when half the working population were unemployed; blackmarketeering and hoarding raised the price of food and thousands went hungry; a phony "land reform" benefited the richer landlords and not the peasants.

Relying on U.S. support, Diem and his family used every means available to suppress opposition. During a reign of terror, special military tribunals were permitted to pass only sentences of death or life imprisonment, and no appeal was allowed. Thousands of innocent people were tortured, imprisoned or executed.

Diem's government was 75 per cent financed by the United States; the army was paid for and equipped by the United States. Only the power of the U.S. stood between Diem and the fury of his people.

When, after eight long and terrible years, the United States at last withdrew its support, Diem was almost immediately assassinated and the people rejoiced.

The successive regimes which followed Diem failed to improve the condition of the people. None was able to establish a government that gained national support.

the N.L.F.

1

2

In 1960, to resist the U.S.-Diem government's ruthless political suppression and gross social injustice the National Liberation Front was formed. It met with immediate response. Within two years it gained control of 80 per cent of the countryside. It developed an armed force (known in the West as the "Viet Cong"). In the areas under its control the N.L.F. divided the land among the peasants, built schools, and brought the beginnings of a medical service to the villages. The President of the N.L.F. was—and is today—Nguyen Huu Tho, a Saigon lawyer, who was imprisoned repeatedly by the French and by the U.S.-Diem regime for his opposition to the foreign-controlled government. Among the members of the Central Committee are Buddhists, Catholics, businessmen, Communists, Socialists, liberal intellectuals and representatives of the peasant organizations and the mountain minority groups.

The N.L.F. issued a ten-point program of surprising moderation. It clearly hoped for widely-based popular support—which it received. The program did not call for immediate re-unification with north Vietnam.

4

5

7

8

SOME LEADING MEMBERS OF THE N.L.F.

1 NGUYEN HUU THO, President of the Central Committee of the N.L.F. Lawyer.
2 YBIH ALEO, Vice President.
3 VO CHI CONG, Vice President.
4 PHUNG VAN CUNG, Vice President. Doctor.
5 THOM ME THE NHEM, Vice President. Buddhist monk.
6 HUYNH TAN PHAT, Vice President. Architect.
7 NGUYEN THI DINH, Deputy-Commander of the Liberation armed forces.
8 NGUYEN VAN NGOI, Eminence Superior of the Cao Dai religion.
9 TRAN VAN THANH, Representative of the N.L.F. in Peking, Trade Unionist.
10 NGUYEN VAN HIEU, Representative of the N.L.F. in Czechoslovakia. Professor.
11 JOSEPH MARIE HO HUE BA, Catholic Priest.
12 THICH HUNG TU, Buddhist monk.

10

11

Members of a mountain minority tribe join the N.L.F. bringing their spears.

Members of the guerrilla forces marching at night.

A member of the women's liberation corps.

At first the guerrillas fought with home-made weapons of the most primitive kind.

Before long they fought with captured weapons—made in the United States.

Members of a villa
“self-defense ur
are given instructi

Schools were started in the areas under the control of the N.L.F.

In the jungle a member of the liberation movement welds fins on to rifle grenades. “For American-made weapons,” says the U.P.I. caption, “ammunition supplies are always available”. The welding equipment was also made in the U.S.A.

American "Advisers"

U.S. operated helicopters used to land Vietnamese troops and to protect them from the air.

Though the number of U.S. troops in Vietnam was continually increasing, the myth that they were there merely as "advisers" was maintained long after anyone anywhere believed it. By 1962 there were 10,000 American troops in Vietnam, but the official line was that they were not involved in the fighting. But newspaper correspondents thought otherwise. "Americans and Vietnamese march together, fight together, and die together," wrote David Halberstam in the N.Y. *Times,* "and it is hard to get much more involved than that."

U. S. Army Ranger advisers teach the fundamentals of hand-to-hand fighting to the Vietnamese.

Instructions being given to Vietnamese troops before they embark in a U.S. helicopter.

Torture—while a U.S. soldier looks on.

"The strange new feature about the photographs c
torture now appearing is that they have been taken wit
the approval of the torturers and published over cap
tions that contain no hint of condemnation. They migh
have come out of a book on insect life. 'The white an
takes certain measures against the red ant after a suc
cessful foray.' But these, after all, are not ants, but men
. . . These photographs are of torturers belonging to a
army which could not exist without American aid an
counsel. . . . The long, slow slide into barbarism of th
Western world seems to have quickened."

GRAHAM GREENE

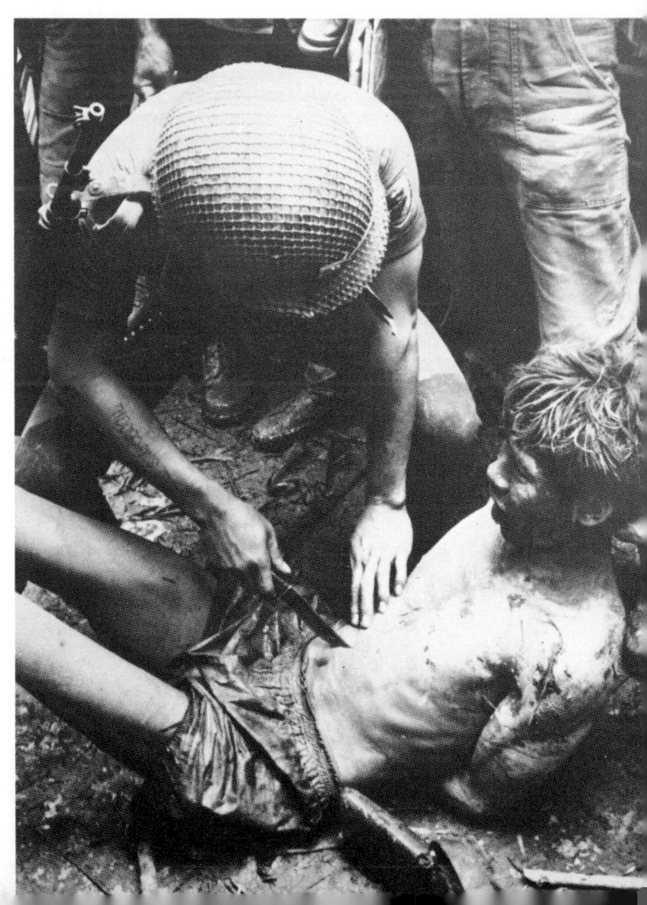

This man, though tortured, refused to speak.
He was shot.

"In more than one case a Vie
Cong suspect has been towe
after interrogation behind an ar
mored personnel carrier. . . . Thi
always results in death in one o
its most painful forms."

MALCOLM BROWNE, in
The New Face of War

Vietnamese attempt to make a suspected guerrilla talk.

A suspected guerrilla is strung up by his feet during interrogation.

A prisoner is given the centuries-old water torture.

U.S. Marines take suspected guerrilla sympathizers back for questioning.

A Marine stands guard.

General Taylor, General Khanh, Secretary of Defense McNamara.

the U.S. moves in big

Constant political unrest in south Vietnam, the ever-increasing number of desertions from the army and the growing disillusionment of the population with the regimes that followed the fall of Diem, led the United States Government to decide that something had to be done to bolster the situation.

By 1963 the decision had been taken in Washington, that the war could not be won unless the United States took a greater hand in the war.

From then on the U.S. commitment of troops and weapons rose sharply.

For the year 1966 the U.S. was planning to drop 638,000 tons of bombs in Vietnam—half the total tonnage *used by the U.S. against the Germans in Europe and Africa in all of World War II.*

BRAVO 1

YL83
YL83

YL71

U.S. ARMY 413121
U.S. ARMY

Unloading cannon from
a helicopter.

Modern equipment moves along a country lane.

Massive weapons with which to fight an elusive enemy.

During battle, one helicopter attempts unsuccessfully to rescue another.

50636

. . . *for we know not what we do.*

the new warfare

Baffled, in spite of its enormous superiority of power, by the lack of military success against the liberation forces, the U.S. looked to other methods which might bring victory. The United States at home was stepping up research and manufacture of arms and equipment for fighting unconventional wars in jungle, mountain, arctic and desert conditions. As Germany and Italy used the Spanish civil war to experiment and try out new weaponry, so the United States began to use what the *Wall Street Journal* called "the ready-made laboratory of South Viet Nam".

Among the weapons that the United States now began to deploy in south Vietnam were toxic sprays against the rice fields; defoliants to strip the jungles of leaves; noxious gases against the civilians; napalm fire bombs to burn up villages; anti-personnel bombs which scatter with incredible force thousands of sharp slivers that tear to shreds any living being within a large area. Sophisticated devices that would assist pilots to detect the presence of human beings far below them in the jungles even at night, highly advanced plane-to-plane missiles, and other refinements of military technology were introduced increasingly into the war in Vietnam.

The sufferers, of course, were the people.

U.S. Air Force C-123's spray defoliants on a south Vietnam jungle.

MARINES

The new "improved" napalm now used in Vietnam contains polystyrene which makes it more "adhesive". The flaming jellied gasoline is impossible to scrape off once it touches the skin.

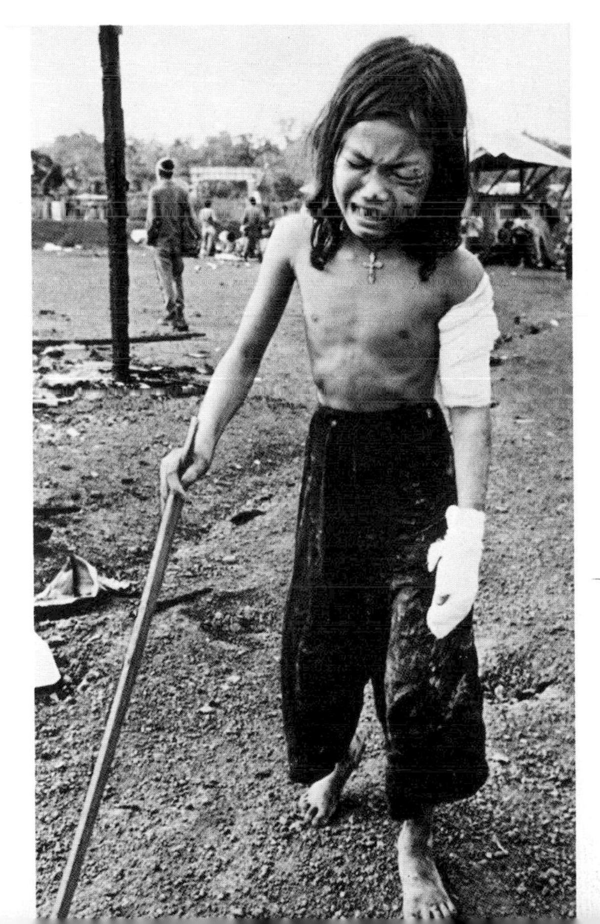

Gas and flame-throwers used in Vietnam.

"Flushing out" (as the caption says), the Vietnamese from their air-raid shelters by the use of "non-lethal" gas. The U.S. government pooh-poohed the significance of using gas. But the N.Y. *Times* reported ". . . even this kind of gas can be fatal to the very young and the very old."

Bombing aftermath.

A "scorched earth" attack. This village was destroyed, the food burned, the livestock killed.

A report presented to Congress indicated that some military actions have resulted in six civilian casualties for every guerrilla killed. The National Liberation Front reported that 170,000 civilians have been killed in south Vietnam and nearly 800,000 have been wounded or disabled by torture. This was in 1965.

"The war in Vietnam is one of the most barbarous wars in history." U THANT

The village of Ba Gia was hit by bombers, rockets and cannon fire in a three day siege.

Two children in the village of Nam Yen
U. S. Marines search for suspects.

The village of Tan An was destroyed by U.S. air strikes during "Operation Masher."

"The United States has the power, if she chooses, to destroy all human life in both parts of Vietnam. But whatever the military outcome of the present war may be, its moral outcome has already been decided . . . America has the ignominious role, whether she wins or loses." ARNOLD TOYNBEE

The innocent victim of a U.S. Marine artillery barrage.

In what previous war in history have aged civilians been trussed, blindfolded, gagged and labelled?

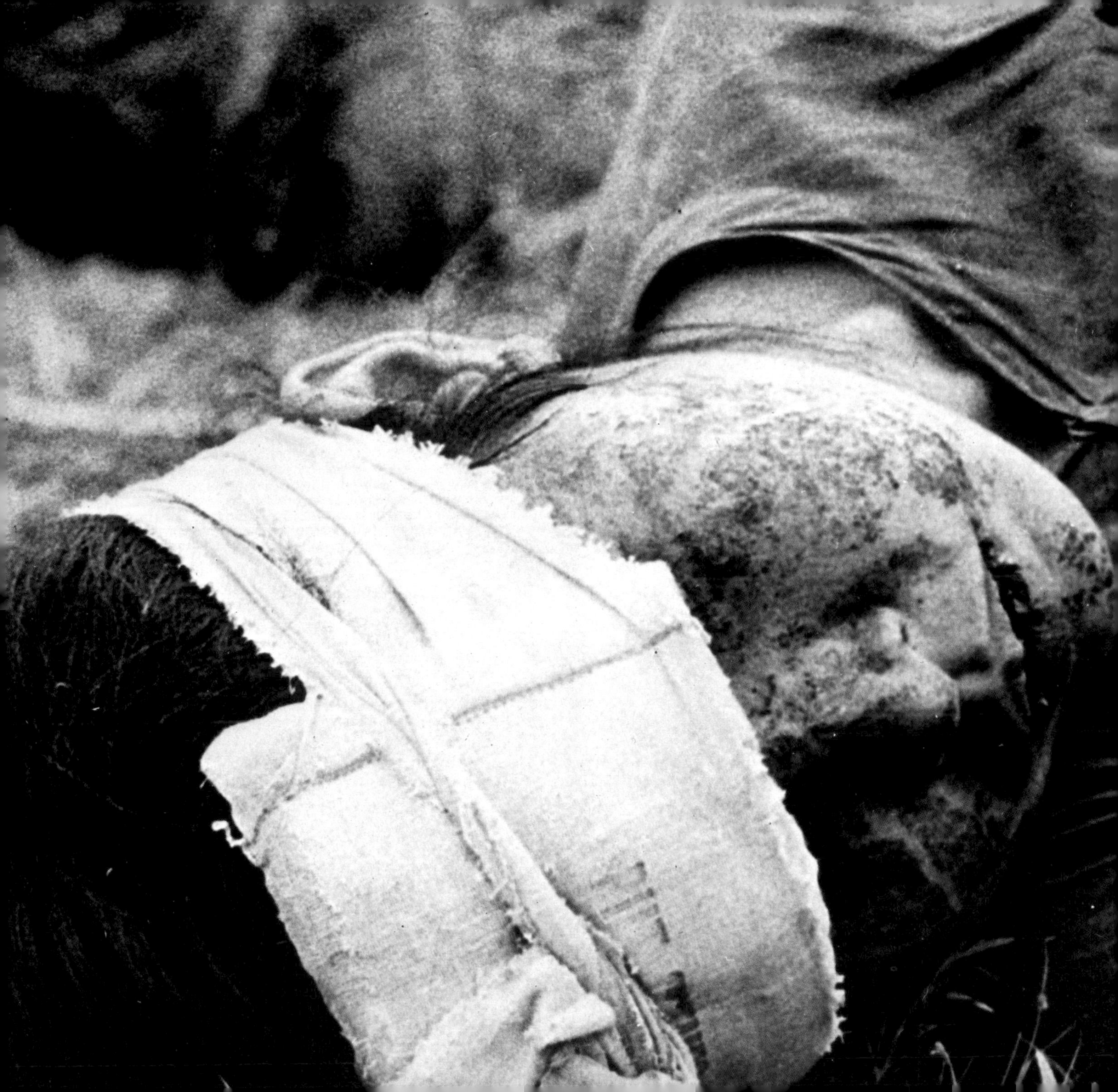

Tanks of the U.S. 173rd Airborne Division on their way to one of the largest operations of the war.

U.S. Marines fire into the smoking rubble of a village hut.

Two girls, 17 and 14, after capture by U.S. paratroopers in a guerrilla training camp.

"They also do a disservice who deny that much has been achieved; that the military program, the economic program, the social program, the informational program, and the technical programs have all accomplished much, have indeed built the springboards of victory." AMBASSADOR HENRY CABOT LODGE

"Humanity is outraged in me and with me. We must not dissimulate nor try to forget this indignation which is one of the most passionate forms of love." GEORGE SAND

Frightened family waits in the fields while troops search the surroundings.

Life must go on.

the war escalates

By early 1965 the situation in south Vietnam was fast disintegrating. Morale in Saigon had sunk to a new low. The desertion rate from the government troops had never been so high. The liberation forces—in spite of all the advanced military equipment now being used against them—still retained the initiative. Washington decided to try to save the situation by breaking out of the frustrating war in the jungles and swamps of south Vietnam—victory, it was thought, might still be possible in the context of a wider war.

On March 2, 1965 the United States Air Force began a systematic round-the-clock bombardment of north Vietnam. A new stage of the Vietnam war had begun.

Secretary of State Rusk defended the bombing of north Vietnam as a way to "stop its aggression of south Vietnam."

The main street of Hanoi, 1965.

the North prepares

Throughout 1965 the bombing of north Vietnam increased in intensity. In a ten-month period there were over 20,000 bombing sorties over north Vietnam—an average of nearly 70 a day. In 1966 the rate of bombing increased even more. Only the cities of Haiphong and the capital, Hanoi, were not subjected to almost constant attacks.

The government of north Vietnam expects that sooner or later Hanoi also will be bombed. Air-raid shelters are being dug along most of the city streets.

The main street of a typical village in north Vietnam.

Ninety-five per cent of the north Vietnamese live in villages such as this, or in scattered hamlets around the rice fields. Many villages have been destroyed in U.S. bombing raids.

No vehicles move along the roads of north Vietnam during the day—even oxcarts going from village to village are liable to be bombed or strafed.

Agricultural methods are primitive by Western standards; there is little rural electrification and even in the cities, industrialization is still in its infancy.

The people of north Vietnam are very determined, very united, and completely certain that they will win—and by "winning" they mean that the United States will remove its military forces from their country and leave them alone.

A formation of F 105s unload their bombs over north Vietnam.

A kindergarten in the provincial town of Nam Dinh south of Hanoi. It was bombed on September 15, 1965. The words above the entrance mean: "Make our children healthy."

What remains of a co-operative worker's apartment house in the centre of the provincial capital of Nam Dinh Province. This city was attacked on July 29, August 2, August 4, and September 15, 1965. Two of the raids were at night.

"Each target", said U.S. Secretary of Defense McNamara on April 26, 1965, "is chosen after a careful review of reconnaissance photographs to ensure that it is isolated and apart from urban populations."

Even young people, such as this sixteen-year old boy, take part in civilian defense—taking messages during air-raids and other liaison work.

Against the bombing raids, the people of north Vietnam have developed a series of defensive measures. In addition to the regular army, a great many civilians have enrolled in what they call "Self Defense" units. When planes fly low, or dive on a village in a strafing attack, they can sometimes be brought down by concentrated fire from rifles fired by the self-defense units. Civilians are also trained in guerrilla warfare techniques in case United States forces should ever attack them on land.

ı "self defense" unit on guard outside
small rural town.

Machine gun posts have been set up near
bridges and other likely targets.

ıti-air craft guns, placed around the
ger towns and the more important
rgets are manned by the regular army.
ıese guns, most of which are not
advanced design, have been supplied
the Chinese, the Soviet Union or
ve been bought from other
cialist countries.

Air raids on north Vietnam are so frequent that even peasants working in the fields often carry rifles with them. At any moment a U.S. plane may zoom out of the clouds on a bombing or strafing attack.

The targets are often of a very trivial nature—such as a small bridge over a country stream. The north Vietnamese military have said: "If the United States wants to defeat us they cannot do so by bombing—they will have to fight us on the ground."

LUC CAC BAN
CHUNG TA DANG

growing opposition in the south

Meanwhile in the south, civilian opposition to the Saigon government and to the United States presence, grew in size and anger. Government troops on innumerable occasions were called out to suppress students, religious groups and others who called for an end to the war.

Nguyen Van Troi, a young electrical worker sentenced to death for an attempt to kill McNamara, spoke to correspondents immediately before his execution in Saigon on October 15, 1964. He was completely self-possessed. "You are journalists," he said, "and so you must be well informed about what is happening. It is the Americans who have committed aggression on our country, it is they who have been killing our people with planes and bombs. . . . I have never acted against the will of my people. It is against the Americans that I have taken action." When a priest wanted to give him absolution he refused, saying: "I have committed no sin. It is the Americans who have sinned." He would not have his eyes covered before execution. "Let me look at our beloved land." He died with the greatest calm. When the first volley hit him he called out: "Long live Vietnam!" Nguyen Van Troi has become a popular hero, in both north and south Vietnam, among those who oppose the United States.

…t police break up …ti-government, …ti-U.S. demonstrations.

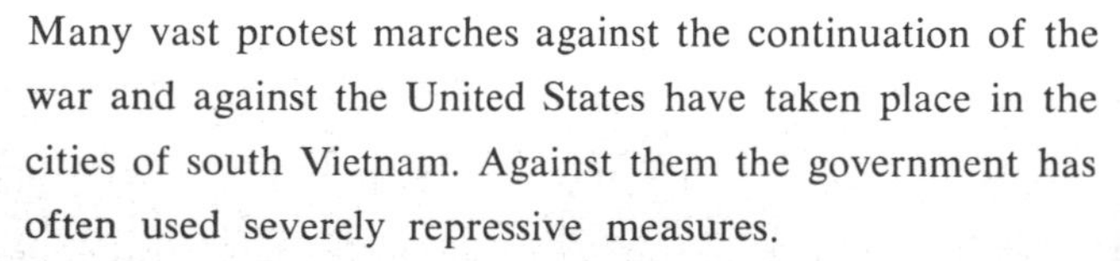

Many vast protest marches against the continuation of the war and against the United States have taken place in the cities of south Vietnam. Against them the government has often used severely repressive measures.

IN VIETNAM'S OWN AFFAIRS

MUA BAN
NỮ TRANG
542 PHAN

SOLEX và XE ĐẠP
SỬA Vespa
hãy làm vật
The Free world

At Danang air base U.S. bombers are made ready for another strike.

". . . our course is resolute, our conviction is firm . . . we shall not be diverted from doing what is necessary in the cause of freedom

PRESIDENT JOHNSON, June 1966

FORCE

The United States and the war in Vietnam

1. Vietnam under the French

VIETNAM, first organized as a state in 208 B.C., suffered in the 19th century, as did so many other Asian countries, the encroachments of Western imperialism. The rapidly growing industries of France demanded both raw materials and markets—and the French colonies in Asia provided both.

In 1858, French troops occupied the country by force, and by 1884 the countries now known as Vietnam, Laos, and Cambodia were firmly under French domination. The French set up a system under which the colony provided the maximum benefit to the French economy regardless of the destructive effect upon the traditional form of society. A small Westernized elite, alienated from the bulk of the peasant population, was cultivated and it was through this local elite that France, backed by its own military forces and colonial officials, ruled the indigenous peoples. The French authority throughout Indochina was absolute.

The peasant population suffered greatly under French rule. Indochina became the third-largest exporter of rice and rubber in the world, but the people remained poor. In 1939 more than a million and a half tons of rice was exported—40 percent of the total production—but the per capita consumption of rice, the region's staple food, had decreased since 1900 by 30 percent. Taxes were heavy and were intended to meet all the costs of the French colonial administration. Much of the taxation was indirect and hit the poorest class of peasants. As in India under the British, the tax on salt became a major source of grievance. The French kept in their own hands the sale of opium, alcohol, tobacco, and salt and, up to World War I, the tax on these commodities alone provided 50 to 60 percent of the colony's revenues.

The plight of the Vietnamese peasants was made worse by the system under which land was owned or used, and by high rent and interest rates. Every year thousands of peasants were thrown off their land because of their inability to meet their debts.

The total effect of French rule on the Vietnamese economy was very damaging. It increased the differences between the wealth of the few and the misery of the many. In the late twenties, rice, coal, and rubber represented three-quarters of the exports, while *three-fifths* of the imports consisted of cars, perfumes, textiles, and domestic items of interest only to the European colonialist and the members of the small Vietnamese elite.

After sixty years of colonial rule, the French were operating 81 prisons—not counting labor camps. Only 2 percent of the children were getting elementary education; only one-half of one percent were going to secondary school; there was one university. In all of Laos, one native doctor had been trained. In 1943 the colonial government spent *five time more* for the purchase of opium (distributed through the official opium monopoly) than for the total combined expenditures on education, libraries, and hospitals.

Such was the legacy of France in Vietnam.

2. Vietnamese Resistance to the French

Throughout the period of French colonial rule, there were constant peasant uprisings, some of which were suppressed with the greatest severity. During World War I, in order to secure the cooperation of the Vietnamese, the French promised to ameliorate their measures of control. As a result, almost 100,000 Vietnamese went to France to serve as soldiers or laborers. The French promises were not kept; conditions in Vietnam after the war were not improved.

Their helplessness under appalling injustices, the ruthless suppression of all opposition, and the arrogance of the French administrators outraged the dignity of the Vietnamese. One Vietnamese who had been to France, later reported:

> "In France I liked the French," he said. "They were *chic* and generous and we had many friends among them. I have happy memories of Frenchmen in France. But Frenchmen here?" He leaned across the table. "I hate them," he said slowly, "with a hatred that must be inconceivable to you, for you have not known what it is to live as a slave under a foreign master."
>
> Harold Isaacs, *No Peace for Asia,* p. 146

Without the cold and desolation of winter
There could not be the warmth and splendor of spring
Calamity has tempered and hardened me
And turned my mind into steel.

Poem by Ho Chi Minh

Among the expatriates in France after the war was a man of twenty-nine, Nguyen Ai Quoc, who was later to be known as Ho Chi Minh. He attempted to rouse the interest of the Versailles Conference in the plight of the Vietnamese. His constant agitation and pamphleteering against the abuses of the French colonial system, and his demands for Vietnamese independence, earned him a strong reputation as a patriot back in Vietnam.

In 1930 and 1931, after several attempted insurrections in Vietnam, the French made a supreme effort to suppress all nationalist parties. The French Legion instituted a nationwide period of "terror." Great numbers of Vietnamese (Communists, nationalists, and liberals) were imprisoned. Thousands of innocent people were executed. Among the provincial administrators who assisted the French in this ruthless attempt to suppress all nationalist groups was a young man called Ngo Dinh Diem, a member of the Vietnamese elite. This same Diem was later to be chosen by the United States Government to become President of south Vietnam.

3. World War II

The Japanese invaded Vietnam in 1940. The French Governor-General offered no resistance and, on order from the Vichy Government (cooperating with Nazi Germany), placed the colony at the disposal of the Japanese. The Japanese administered Vietnam through the French colonial bureaucracy, who supplied the Japanese forces with rice and conscripted native labor for them. In 1945, not long before Japan's defeat, the Japanese rid themselves of the French. They set up Bao Dai, a Vietnamese aristocrat, as a puppet "Emperor" and for a few months administered Vietnam through him.

All over Asia flutter the anti-Japanese flags:
Big flags or little flags—they are not all the same
Of course. Big flags we must have, but we need the little flags, too.
Poem by Ho Chi Minh

During the Japanese occupation, a secret coalition was formed of all groups struggling for Vietnamese independence—"The League for Independence of Vietnam," referred to by many Western writers as the "Viet Minh." Ho Chi Minh was the founder. The "Viet Minh" carried on increasingly strong activity under the slogan: NEITHER THE FRENCH NOR THE JAPANESE AS MASTERS! FOR THE INDEPENDENCE OF VIETNAM!

The Independence Movement, under Ho Chi Minh's leadership, cooperated with the United States and with those French not under German domination, on the basis of joint action against Japanese fascism. When, on August 14, the Japanese surrendered, there was no doubt in the minds of Ho Chi Minh and all the Vietnamese nationalists that now, at long last, their country's independence was at hand.

4. Vietnam's Declaration of Independence

On September 2, 1945, in Hanoi, Ho Chi Minh read out to a vast cheering crowd the Vietnamese "Declaration of Independence." The Vietnamese had for long and bitter years fought for their independence against a foreign colonial power. It was natural for them to recall a similar declaration signed by the Americans 169 years earlier.

The Vietnam "Declaration of Independence" is worth rereading:

"All men are created equal. They are endowed by their Creator with certain inalienable rights, among these are Life, Liberty, and the pursuit of Happiness."

This immortal statement was made in the Declaration of Independence of the United States of America in 1776. In a broader sense, this means: All the peoples on earth are equal from birth, all the peoples have a right to live, to be happy and free . . .

Nevertheless, for more than eighty years, the French imperialists, abusing the standard of Liberty, Equality, and Fraternity, have violated our Fatherland and oppressed our fellow citizens . . .

They have enforced inhuman laws; they have set up three distinct political regimes in the north, the center, and the south of Vietnam in order to wreck our national unity and to prevent our people from becoming united.

They have built more prisons than schools. They have mercilessly slain our patriots; they have drowned our uprisings in rivers of blood. They have fettered public opinion; they have practiced obscurantism against our people. To weaken our race they have forced us to use opium and alcohol.

In the fields of economics they have fleeced us to our backbone, impoverished our people, and devastated our land.

They have robbed us of our rice fields, our mines, our forests, our raw materials. They have monopolized the issuing of bank-notes and the export trade.

They have invented numerous unjustifiable taxes and reduced our people, especially our peasantry, to a state of extreme poverty . . .

The French have fled, the Japanese have capitulated, Emperor Bao Dai has abdicated. Our people have broken the chains which for nearly a century have fettered them and have won independence for the Fatherland . . .

For these reasons, we, members of the Provisional Government of the Democratic Republic of Vietnam, solemnly declare to the world that Vietnam has the right to be a free and independent country—and in fact is so already. The entire Vietnamese people are determined to mobilize all their physical and mental strength, to sacrifice their lives and property in order to safeguard their independence and liberty.

5. The Independence Sabotaged

At the moment when Ho Chi Minh was reading the Declaration of Independence to the crowds in Hanoi, the authority of the new Republic extended over the whole territory of Vietnam. Never before had the people of Vietnam been so united and independent. It was not to last long.

South of the 16th parallel, the British Army was taking the surrender of the Japanese forces. They immediately released the French who had been imprisoned by the Vietnamese for collaborating with the Japanese. The British were already attempting to re-establish French rule. "I was welcomed on arrival [at Saigon] by Viet Minh," reported General Gracey, commander of the British forces; "I promptly kicked them out." Independence in Saigon lasted just three weeks.

In the north, the French officers were openly contemptuous of the Vietnamese. They referred to the liberation troops, the "Viet Minh," as *les jaunes*—the yellow ones. On March 6, 1946, the French signed an agreement with Ho Chi Minh granting Vietnam independence within the framework of the French Union. It soon became clear that the French were not prepared to honor this agreement. On November 23, in a move to regain their military position in Vietnam, the French bombarded the port of Haiphong and Ho Chi Minh called the people of Vietnam to arms to defend their new Republic. He also appealed to the people of the world for peace based on the agreement that had been made with the French; but the appeal was ignored by the French, who hoped to re-establish their former colonial control.

Early in 1947 French troops moved in and occupied Hanoi. The Vietnamese, after a series of defeats due to French superiority in equipment and numbers, once more turned to guerrilla warfare.

The struggle for independence was on again in earnest.

6. The United States Comes to the Assistance of the French

"I would hate very much to see us involved in a land war in Asia. I think we would be fighting a wrong war at the wrong place against the wrong enemy."

General Omar Bradley

The French officers who had spoken with such contempt of *les jaunes* found that they were attacking a well-organized army—an army backed by the concerted effort of all the Vietnamese people. Between 1947 and 1954 France increased her forces until 250,000 Frenchmen were fighting in Vietnam.

The United States was now taking an active interest in the war in Vietnam.

The success of the Chinese revolution in 1949 had altered the balance of power throughout the Far East. Dulles by this time had developed his policy of "containment" and it was the pursuance of this policy that led the United States to support the French military effort.

The United States was at first hesitant to intervene—it did not wish to be seen supporting the re-establishment of French colonialism. By 1950 a solution to this quandary was found. France granted "independence" to Vietnam, installing Bao Dai (the former puppet emperor under the Japanese—a man utterly detested by his people) as "President." The real purpose of this move was obvious. As Eden, the British Foreign Secretary, wrote in his memoirs: "The United States was now able to help the French with arms and money without bolstering colonialism."

It was a "phantom state" which France set up and vested with the legal attributes of "independence." But it served its purpose. From then on the French were able to redefine their war as a "crusade against Communism" and Vietnam became the "barrier against Communism" in Southeast Asia. France now presented itself, not as a colonial power attempting to re-establish its rule over a subject people, but as the "sentinel of the free world" taking on the burden of protecting Bao Dai's "free Vietnam" from the "Red" tide.

This was precisely what the United States wanted.

In 1950, the U.S. established a Military and Advisory Group (MAAG) in Vietnam and the first shipment of U.S. arms arrived on August 10. Between this date and the defeat of the French at Dien Bien Phu in 1954 the American taxpayers were to foot 80 percent of the cost of the war, thus allowing the French (with all the suffering it caused the Vietnamese people) to continue a struggle they would otherwise have had to abandon much sooner.

> "I am against sending American G.I.'s into the mud and muck of Indochina on a blood-letting spree to perpetuate colonialism and white man's exploitation in Asia."
>
> Senator Lyndon B. Johnson, April 1954

The United States was not, however, so much interested in re-establishing the French in Vietnam as in extending its own authority in this area. President Eisenhower on August 4, 1953, told a conference of U.S. state governors in Seattle:

> Now let us assume that we lost Indochina . . . The tin and tungsten that we so greatly value from that area would cease coming . . . So when the United States votes 400 million dollars to help that war, we are not voting a give-away program. We are voting for the cheapest way that we can to prevent the occurrence of something that would be of a most terrible significance to the United States of America, our security, our power and ability to get certain things we need from the riches of the Indochinese territory and from Southeast Asia.

Secretary of State Dulles on March 29, 1954, said:

> It is rich in many raw materials such as tin, oil, rubber and iron ore . . . The area has great strategic value . . . It has major naval and air bases.

U.S.News & World Report of April 4, 1954, ran an article under the title, "Why U.S. Risks War for Indochina: It's the Key to Control of All Asia." In it the following statement appeared:

> One of the world's richest areas is open to the winner in Indochina. That's behind the growing U.S. concern . . . tin, rubber, rice, key strategic raw materials are what the war is really about. The U.S. sees it as a place to hold—at any cost.

As events in the next few years would show, justifications for "helping the French" were hypocritical. They appealed to the hard-headed American voter but obscured the long-term objective. The support of the French, and the setting up of MAAG, were only steps toward the control of Vietnam by the United States itself. A more recent and more candid revelation of U.S. motives was made by Henry Cabot Lodge, now Ambassador to south Vietnam, in an address before the Middlesex Club of Cambridge, and reported in the Boston *Sunday Globe* on February 28, 1965:

> Geographically, Vietnam stands at the hub of a vast area of the world—Southeast Asia—an area with a population of 249 million persons . . . He who holds or has influence in Vietnam can affect the future of the Philippines and Formosa to the east, Thailand and Burma with their huge rice surpluses to the west, and Malaysia and Indonesia with their rubber, ore and tin to the south . . . Vietnam thus does not exist in a geographical vacuum—from it large storehouses of wealth and population can be influenced and undermined [*sic*].

7. Resistance by the Vietnamese

To the people of Vietnam, the prospect of the French re-establishing their colonial rule was intolerable. They were ready to sacrifice their lives to prevent it. Even with massive U.S. military aid, the French found (as the U.S. was to find ten years later) that to fight a determined peasant population is not easy. The strength of the liberation troops lay in their close identification with the peasants. On April 5, 1948, Ho Chi Minh issued an order to his troops which he called "Twelve Recommendations." These "Recommendations" issued to his troops indicate vividly the kind of grass-roots war the resistance movement was engaged in.

TWELVE RECOMMENDATIONS

Six Forbiddances

1. *Not to do what is likely to damage the land and crops or spoil the houses and belongings of the people.*
2. *Not to insist on buying or borrowing what the people are not willing to sell or lend.*
3. *Not to bring hens into mountainous people's houses.*
4. *Never to break our word.*
5. *Not to give offense to people's faith and customs (such as to lie down before the altar, to raise feet over the hearth, to play music in the house, etc.).*
6. *Not to do or speak what is likely to make people believe that we hold them in contempt.*

Six Permissibles

1. *To help the people in their daily work (harvesting, fetching firewood, carrying wood, sewing, etc.).*

North Americans consume nearly five times as much food per person as do the peoples of Asia. American women spend more each year on cosmetics than the total national budgets of all the new African states combined.

"The penalty of affluence is that it cuts one off from the common lot, common experience and common fellowship. In a sense it outlaws one automatically from one's human birthright of membership in the great human family."

Arnold Toynbee

2. *Whenever possible to buy commodities for those who live far from markets (knife, salt, needle, thread, paper, pen, etc.).*
3. *In spare time to tell amusing, simple, and short stories useful to the Resistance, but not to betray secrets.*
4. *To teach the people the national script and elementary hygiene.*
5. *To study the customs of each region so as to be acquainted with them in order to create an atmosphere of sympathy, then gradually to explain to the people to abate their superstitions.*
6. *To show to the people that you are correct, diligent, and disciplined.*

Characteristically, Ho Chi Minh finished this order to his troops with a poem:

The above mentioned twelve recommendations
Are feasible to all.
He who loves his country
Will never forget them.
When the people have a habit,
All are like one man,
With good army men and good people,
Everything will be crowned with success.
Only when the root is firm, can the tree live long,
And victory is built with the people as foundations.

8. Dien Bien Phu—Defeat Of the French

In spite of massive support from the U.S. and the deployment in Vietnam of many of their finest troops, the French, by the spring of 1954, were facing defeat.

The final crisis came at Dien Bien Phu where the French were hoping to bring the liberation forces to fight in open battle, but where instead they themselves were trapped. The siege—followed breathlessly by the whole world—began on March 13. All supplies had to be air-lifted to the encircled garrison. On May 7, after eight weeks of bitter fighting, the French surrendered. With the defeat at Dien Bien Phu, French military influence in Southeast Asia was brought to an end.

It has become fashionable today, in an attempt to diminish the extraordinary heroism and military skill of the Vietnamese, to say that the defeat of the French was the result of national weariness at home—that the war "was lost in Paris." There is little evidence to support this. Whatever doubts about the war were being voiced in France, and there were many, the French troops in Vietnam continued until the end to fight with extreme tenacity.

"Anybody who commits the land power of the United States on the continent of Asia ought to have his head examined."

General Douglas MacArthur

The French lost the war in Vietnam because they were attempting to impose an unjust political settlement by military means. The Vietnamese were fighting on their own soil for their own freedom. As the Americans showed in their own war of independence, power in defense of freedom is always greater than power mobilized on behalf of oppression.

9. Geneva

The conference held at Geneva in 1954 was an attempt to settle once and for all the political problems resulting from the end of French colonial rule in Indochina.

There were nine participants: the Democratic Republic of Vietnam, Cambodia, Laos, the People's Republic of China, the Soviet Union, France, Great Britain, the United States, and the "State of Vietnam" (the Bao Dai regime). Diametrically opposed forces with deeply conflicting objectives faced each other across the conference table.

The first month saw the conference stalled, lost in formalities, the delegates dragging their feet. The situation was made more difficult by the actions of the American delegation who made it clear that they were opposed to *any* settlement that would give independence to a united Vietnam, and they treated the conference as having no real significance. Writing to Winston Churchill during the conference, Anthony Eden, the British representative, said: "The Chinese . . . have all along suspected that the Americans intend to intervene in Indochina whatever arrangements we try to arrive at here." Events were to prove that the Chinese suspicions were fully justified.

On June 8 the deadlock was broken when the representatives of the government in Hanoi put forward proposals which represented far-reaching concessions. They offered to agree to the temporary separation of the northern and southern zones of Vietnam and were ready to accept control over only about half of Vietnam territory, though they were then exercising control over three-quarters of it. These concessions were made only on certain very clearly defined conditions:

1. That the administrative separation of north and south at the 17th parallel was provisional and was in no way to be construed as a permanent division of Vietnam.
2. That elections would be held within two years to assure the unification of the country.

3. That neither zone would meanwhile make international alliances or receive military help from the outside.

These points were accepted by all members of the conference with the exception of the United States and the so-called Bao Dai regime. Though not accepting the agreements, the United States delegate gave a solemn undertaking not to disturb them by force or the threat of force.

Just two days after the conclusion of this conference (a conference pledged to secure the unification of Vietnam) Dulles declared that one of the good aspects of the conference was that it "advanced the independent status of . . . South Vietnam" and that the important thing was to "prevent the loss of northern Vietnam from leading to the extension of Communism throughout Southeast Asia."

So much for Dulles' intention to fulfill the terms of the Geneva Conference!

Dulles was not alone. Hardly had the conference ended when the French Government announced it would continue to recognize the Bao Dai regime as the sole trustee of Vietnam sovereignty; this ended all possibility of political cooperation between Paris and Hanoi.

"It was with you, the French, that we signed the Geneva Agreements," declared the Prime Minister of the Democratic Republic, "and it is up to you to see that they are respected." But France had pulled out.

Thus, north Vietnam, having made major territorial and political concessions at Geneva, found herself cheated by the West.

Under provisions of the Geneva Conference, nearly 900,000 Vietnamese living in the northern zone now moved south. (A smaller number living in the southern zone moved north.) This movement to the south has repeatedly been cited to show the unpopularity of the government in Hanoi; that these refugees "voted with their feet."

What is often not said is that 600,000 of those who left the north were Catholics. Of the non-Catholic population of north Vietnam, 98 percent remained where they were. What must also be remembered is that a large number of these Catholics had actively collaborated with the French against their own countrymen—and fearing punishment moved south. The Catholic migration to the south was

> admittedly the result of an extremely intensive . . . very successful American psychological warfare operation. Propaganda slogans and leaflets appealed to the devout Catholics with such themes as "Christ has gone to the South" and "The Virgin Mary has departed from the North."
>
> Bernard Fall, *The Two Viet-Nams,* p. 153

10. The U.S. Chooses Diem

While the conference was still in session at Geneva, the U.S. Government took steps to ensure that its own nominee was appointed to head the government in south Vietnam. Dulles told the French that if they wished to retain any influence in Vietnam they must order Bao Dai to appoint Ngo Dinh Diem as Prime Minister. This was done. Soon thereafter, following a farcical "plebiscite" (even *Time* described the referendum as "rigged"), Diem ousted Bao Dai and was established as "President, Prime Minister, and Minister of Defense" of the "Republic of Vietnam" with the full backing of the United States.

How did the United States come to select Diem (the same Diem who earlier in his career had helped the French suppress the independence movement) as the man to protect its interests?

Diem was a Catholic and a member of the Vietnamese aristocracy. Two years after the French, in 1931, had attempted and failed to suppress the nationalist movement in Vietnam, Diem went into retirement. He was then thirty-three years old. His turn came again in 1950 when he came to the United States to plead his cause for a reformed Vietnam under an anti-French, anti-Communist government. His brother, Bishop Can, was an important contact with the American Catholic Church, and Cardinal Spellman soon became one of Diem's many important admirers. *Look* magazine (January 28, 1964) was to write of Diem:

> Secretary of State John Foster Dulles picked him, Sen. Mike Mansfield endorsed him, Francis Cardinal Spellman praised him, Vice-President Richard M. Nixon liked him, and President Dwight D. Eisenhower O.K.'d him.

From the moment that the U.S. Government selected Diem, without any consultation with the Vietnamese people, to act for it in south Vietnam the United States found itself drawn inexorably, step by step, into an ever widening morass. Looking back, we can only wonder at the blindness of those American leaders who could bring themselves to believe that a wealthy, absentee aristocrat, an ex-member of the French colonial administration, could impose his rule upon the Vietnamese people without arousing enormous popular opposition.

By selecting and continuing to support Ngo Dinh Diem as head of the south Vietnam government, the U.S. linked its vast authority, its treasure, and its honor to the whims and dictates of a tyrant. Diem would not have lasted a day if the U.S. had not given him its unstinted support with arms, money, and praise. When, after eight long and terrible years, the U.S. finally withdrew its support, Diem was immediately hounded down and shot and the people went wild with rejoicing.

> "The fears and passions of idealogical conflict have diverted the minds and energies of our people from the constructive tasks of a free society to a morbid preoccupation with the dangers of communist aggression abroad, and subversion and disloyalty at home."
>
> Senator J. William Fulbright

11. The Struggle for Reunification

Diem's appointment signaled the start of a new phase in American involvement in Vietnam. The U.S. did not feel bound by the agreements made at Geneva, and through Diem soon showed that it had no intention of allowing the elections promised at Geneva.

On February 4, 1955, the government in Hanoi proposed the restoration of normal relations between the northern and southern zones, for mail services, roads, railways, air and sea traffic, and so on. This proposal was rejected. (Today the 17th parallel remains one of the most closely sealed borders in the world.)

Hanoi also in 1955 urged the south to take part in a consultative conference (as provided for at Geneva) to arrange details of the 1956 nationwide elections. This was rejected. Repeatedly, in May and June 1956, in July 1957, in March 1958, in July 1959, and in July 1960, the government in Hanoi urged Diem to agree to a pre-election conference, offering to negotiate on the basis of "free elections by secret ballot." Each time the proposal was met with a scornful silence or a stinging reply.

The reason why the U.S. refused to allow elections was abundantly clear. No one who knew the conditions in Vietnam was in any doubt that, if elections were held, Ho Chi Minh would be elected by an overwhelming majority of the people.

> I have never talked or corresponded with a person knowledgeable in Indochinese affairs who did not agree that had elections been held . . . possibly 80 per cent of the population would have voted for the Communist Ho Chi Minh.
>
> President Eisenhower, *Mandate for Change,* p. 372

In an attempt to justify the U.S. refusal to allow elections, the State Department in its 1961 Blue Book on Vietnam, said that elections (not mentioning that they were an essential provision of the Geneva Agreement and were to have been internationally supervised) were a "well-laid trap" which would "turn all of south Vietnam over to the Communists."

> "The reason why the Vietcong will not suffer a political defeat is because . . . they are still closer to the people, more aware of Vietnamese problems, more conscious of national dignity and independence than any regime to come out of Saigon."
>
> *The Times* (London), March 24, 1966

> As early as September 1954 it became clear that the Americans' desire to hold on to the 17th parallel at all costs, would constitute a serious obstacle to the reunification of Vietnam. The latter was in danger of being sacrificed to the demands of the Pentagon world strategy.
>
> Philippe Devillers, *China Quarterly,* No. 9 (January-March, 1962), p. 4

The primary feature of the Geneva Agreements was the recognition that Vietnam was *one* country and *one* people. At the time of Geneva both the government in Hanoi and the Bao Dai regime in Saigon were claiming sovereignty over the whole country. The Geneva Conference itself made no pronouncement on this question. It specifically deferred the matter to July 1956, when the Vietnamese people themselves, at a general election, would determine which government they preferred.

By its rejection of elections, the United States effectively sabotaged the intensions of the Geneva Agreements, and from that moment the myth of "two Vietnams" was to be carefully cultivated by apologists for American policies.

12. The Nature of Diem's Rule

> When President Diem took over in 1955 his authority did not extend beyond the Presidential Palace.
>
> Leland Burrows, Head of U.S.O.M. Saigon, May 1957, in a conversation reported by William Warbey, M.P.

In Vietnam there had been strong opposition when Diem's appointment was first announced, but on November 17, 1954, General Collins, who was President Eisenhower's special representative in south Vietnam, issued an ultimatum: the south Vietnamese army would receive no more American aid unless it supported Diem *(Keesing's Contemporary Archives,* Nov. 17, 1954, p. 14949). The army made no further protest.

Once installed and conscious of complete backing by the U.S., Diem moved to consolidate his position by the suppression of all opposition. At first his opponents were denounced as the "leftovers" from the French colonial regime. After 1956 every opponent was called a Communist. The Diem regime came more and more to reflect the worst features of a colonial administration.

> The Diem Government . . . launched . . . what amounted to a series of manhunts. . . . This repression was in theory aimed at the Communists. In fact it affected all those, and there were many, democrats, socialists, liberals . . . who were bold enough to express their disagreement with . . . the ruling oligarchy . . .
>
> In 1958 the situation grew worse. Round-ups of "dissidents" became more frequent and more brutal . . . A certain sequence of events became almost classical: denunciation, encirclement of villages, searches and raids, arrest of suspects, plundering, interrogations enlivened sometimes by torture (even of innocent people), deportation . . .
>
> Diem never succeeded in winning the peasants and tenant farmers over to his side.
>
> Philippe Devillers, *China Quarterly,* No. 9 (January-March, 1962), pp. 12-13

In 1959, Diem passed the celebrated Law 10/59 under which special military tribunals were set up to try "infringements of national security." The tribunals were expressly forbidden to allow extenuating circumstances. They were permitted to pass only sentences of death or hard labor for life. Under this law, no appeal was possible.

The New York *World-Telegram* revealed that merely "the *intention* to shake one's fist in the direction of the Presidential Palace" made one liable to punishment by the military tribunal. Thousands during this period were executed, or were herded into concentration camps and kept under the most appalling conditions.

By this time, Diem's atrocities were attracting international attention and many organizations abroad were demanding an inquiry. These were invariably refused.

"What is happening in Vietnam is sickening, and is bound to make the U.S.A. a deeply hated nation in Asia for decades to come."

The Economic Weekly, Bombay

In April 1960 eighteen highly respected Vietnamese, of varying political affiliations, demanded that Diem liberalize his regime. If he did not, they said, a revolution would follow. Their demand elicited no response.

Even among those most strongly opposed to Communism, opposition to Diem's ruthless dictatorship grew more bitter month by month.

> This rising is justified: In a country where the most elementary rights of the people are ignored, where the legality of the actions of the government has become an empty expression, the will of the people can only make itself felt by means of a revolution.
>
> *Pour le Viet-Nam* (Paris), November 2, 1960

Even in the army the mood of the officers became hostile to the regime, and on November 11, 1960, a military coup d'etat was attempted. It failed, and was followed by a large-scale purge. The U.S. was still determined to maintain Diem in power.

Not only was the U.S.–Diem rule politically repressive, but it failed to tackle any of the more urgently needed social reforms. American aid, on which the economy became more and more dependent, reduced, rather than enhanced, the employment of local labor. By 1962, according to official statistics, almost 50 percent of the potential workers in south Vietnam were unemployed. Destitution was widespread. Though housing and hospitals were desperately needed for the poorer people, building resources were mostly used for the construction of high-rent villas and apartments and for amusement centers. Between 1957 and 1960 only 7,656 square yards of hospitals were built, but 56,000 square yards of dance halls and movie theatres were erected. There was almost no low-rent construction for the poor.

It is generally assumed that the U.S. presence in Vietnam—whatever other difficulties it may create—at least is of economic benefit to the country. The reverse is actually true. The presence of large numbers of Americans seriously dislocates the Vietnamese economy. It is estimated that $200,000,000 will be spent by U.S. servicemen in south Vietnam in 1966. This will mostly benefit taxicab owners, bars, prostitutes, hotel keepers, and restaurant proprietors. ("Both literally and figuratively," Senator Fulbright said, "Saigon has become an American brothel.") The ordinary Vietnamese people derive almost no benefit from this expenditure, but suffer considerable hardship. The heavy additional demand for consumer goods cannot be met and drives up the cost of living. In the single month of January 1966 the cost-of-living index rose 11 percent. In spite of rice imports from the U.S. (to a country that formerly exported rice!), the price rose 50 percent in one year, with many merchants hoarding the supplies hoping for the price to rise still more. For a people with only a very slender margin of security, these price rises have been a disaster.

Ninety percent of the south Vietnamese people do not live in the cities, but are peasants living on the land.

Even after a so-called 'land reform' 2 percent of the population of south Vietnam own 45 percent of the land.

The U.S.–Diem regime's greatest failure was its refusal to carry through any genuine redistribution of the land. Land reform, such as it was, turned out to favor the landlords rather than the peasants. Describing this, Dennis Warner, the noted Australian correspondent, wrote that under Diem's so-called land reform:

> A landlord in south Vietnam may retain up to a hundred hectares of rice land [about 270 acres]. . . . To have been cut down to this level may have been unpleasant for the rich; but it was precious little to help the poor in a country where half a million peasant families own farms of one hectare or less.
>
> The program lacked regulatory machinery . . . and all sorts of side arrangements were entered into to defeat its intention. . . . In practice, the system usually works as yet another means for squeeze and graft by appointed village chiefs and one of the worst forms of land exploitation. No security of tenure is given [to the peasants] beyond the crop year.
>
> *The Last Confucian*, p. 116

At the time of the collapse of French authority, many of the rich landlords fled to the safety of the cities. When, several years later, under the U.S.–Diem regime, they thought it safe to return to the country, they demanded that the peasants pay them *back rent* for the years that they had been away. Rent was normally 50 percent of the crop, so some landlords who had been away for eight years demanded 400 percent. It was, of course, impossible to pay 400 percent of a crop. Landlords in this way were able to evict peasants from their land and thus re-establish their former estates.

No wonder the peasants resisted this basically phony "land reform"—especially those who had lived in areas under the control of the Liberation Movement, where all rents had been abolished.

13. The Origins of the National Liberation Front

It is against this background of ruthless political repression and gross social injustice that we must understand the setting up in December 1960 of the "National Front of Liberation of South Vietnam."

It met with immediate and widespread support. Within two years it gained control of 80 percent of the countryside. It set up administrative organizations and committees throughout the south; it developed an armed force (which is often referred to in the West as the "Vietcong"). The popular support given the N.L.F. forced the governing regime to fall back on the principal cities and the main lines of communications.

The N.L.F., as a resistance movement, instituted land-reform programs in areas where the territory it held was secure; it built schools; it started a banking and postal system; and it took on increasingly the administrative responsibilities of organized government. One of its leaders was Nguyen Huu Tho, a Saigon lawyer. Among its thirty-one-member central committee were Buddhists, Catholics, businessmen, Communists, Socialists, liberal intellectuals, and representatives of the peasant organizations and the mountain minority groups.

The National Liberation Front issued a ten-point program (included later in this book) of surprising moderation. The Front was clearly hoping for widely based popular support—which it received. It did not call for immediate reunification with the north, but suggested that this should be accomplished in progressive stages on the basis of negotiation between the two zones, and that meanwhile the two zones would promise not to engage in military or propaganda activities likely to lead to tension. They would encourage economic and cultural exchanges between north and south, freedom of travel and trade, and the opening of the postal services. All this was prudent and restrained enough.

Resistance by the N.L.F. was not the only danger threatening the United States in Vietnam. Others, less obvious, were just as grave. Nepotism and graft were among them. Diem's appointment of his immediate family to high office, the widespread black-market racketeering, the prevailing atmosphere of corruption and depravity, all helped to alienate even those who were appalled at the prospects of a Communist victory. In a country as proudly nationalist as Vietnam the close association of the U.S. with this regime helped to undermine popular support and hastened its end. Reports of the eulogies showered upon Diem by American spokesmen in the U.S. drifted back to Vietnam, aggravating the sense of helplessness and fury of those who opposed him and undercutting the efforts of those who might otherwise have brought pressure upon him to ameliorate his cruelties.

While the U.S.–Diem regime was conducting its pitiless witch hunts in the south, while thousands were being executed or herded into concentration camps, the United States Government continued, almost until the last moment before Diem was assassinated, to tell the people of America that their man in Vietnam was fighting heroically for peace and liberty.

> "The tragedy of Britain in 1775 was that it linked itself with the counter revolution—the Galloways, the colonial governors, the great landholders—rather than the Adams and the Sons of Liberty. The tragedy of the United States, 191 years later, is that it hasn't learned from its own history, for it is now aligned with the counter revolution in Vietnam."
>
> Sidney Lens, *Liberation*, February 1966

In 1957, in welcoming Diem to New York City, Mayor Wagner described him as "a man to whom freedom is the very breath of life." At a banquet in New York, Diem was presented with an award for "inspired leadership in the cause of the free world."

President Eisenhower spoke of Diem's "inspiring leadership in the cause of the free world" and said that it was "opening up vast arcas for the peaceful progress of mankind."

The New York *Times* described Diem as "a man of deep religious heart." *Life* said, "Diem is respected today for the miracles he has wrought."

Secretary of State Dulles said he was much impressed by Prime Minister Diem: "He is a true patriot, dedicated to independence and to the enjoyment by his people of political and religious freedoms."

And to cap everything, Vice-President Lyndon B. Johnson in 1961 acclaimed Diem as "The Churchill of Vietnam."

Thus were the American people led to believe that Diem was worthy of their moral support and of the enormous financial and military aid that alone protected him from the fury of his people.

14. Growing United States Involvement

Despite the glowing tributes to Diem voiced in America, conditions in south Vietnam moved from bad to worse. All attempts to suppress the liberation movement only increased its strength.

In May 1961 the United States Government realized some new ideas were needed which would stand a better chance of success. Vice-President Johnson and relays of other officials were dispatched to Vietnam to see what could be done. The new plans, when they emerged, were these: The U.S. would increase Diem's forces to 600,000; 16,000 "strategic hamlets" were to be set up to "separate the Vietcong from the people"; trees were to be defoliated so that the guerrillas could conceal themselves less effectively; and the U.S. "advisers" were to be given operational control in a generally stepped-up campaign against the liberation forces to bring them to their knees.

For a short while, a mood of optimism prevailed in Washington. Here, at least, were some plans—it was a relief to have something concrete to work with. The new orders went out. With the U.S. army taking over operational control things would obviously improve. Mr. McNamara was sufficiently carried away to say (rashly) that the troops would soon be coming home.

The new mood quickly evaporated. The bright, hopeful plans almost at once began to go wrong and nothing developed as expected. The Vietnamese army was enlarged, but the desertion rate went up even more. The liberation forces, far from losing the initiative, gained strength, both in numbers and in equipment—most of which they had captured. It became clear that the massive quantities of American weapons being pumped into Vietnam benefited the guerrillas more than the government forces. Despite an enormous propaganda effort, there was no increase of popular enthusiasm for Diem. Attempts to bribe or cajole men into his armed services were not successful, and force had to be used to press-gang them.

As for the "strategic hamlets" plan, it met with immediate hostility from the peasants.

> Supposedly the purpose of the fortified villages is to keep the Vietcong out. But the barbed wire denies entrance and exit. Vietnamese farmers are forced at gun-point into these virtual concentration camps. Their homes, possessions, and crops are burned.
>
> Dallas *Morning News,* January 1, 1963

So great was the resistance to these hamlets that in many instances the peasants took matters into their own hands. Of 8,000 strategic hamlets, 80 percent were demolished by the people. Some had to be rebuilt as many as sixty times. By mid-1963 even *Time,* a staunch supporter of a hard policy in Vietnam, conceded that "the peasants strongly resist the plea for strategic hamlets into which they are herded by force." By October it was generally concluded that the program had been a huge flop.

The stepped-up military activity included the use of a number of new weapons. As the U.S. entered increasingly into actual military combat, the nature of the fighting altered. Vietnam became the testing ground for a great variety of weapons that had been developed in the United States but required testing under combat conditions.

> "In Vietnam gas was supplied and sanctioned by white men against Asians. This is something that no Asian, Communist or not, will forget."
>
> Editorial in the New York *Times*

The use of toxic sprays and gases brought international opposition, but after a pause to let the "static" die down the use of these weapons was again authorized. As a result, many people, and thousands of buffaloes, oxen, pigs, and fowl were killed. Thousands of acres of rice crops were destroyed. The reasoning behind this was that if the peasants were short of food, they would be less likely to have any to spare to give to the guerrilla forces.

No one in the U.S. Government would yet concede that the United States was involved as a combatant. The myth that the thousands of U.S. troops in Vietnam were merely "advisers" was officially maintained long after no one anywhere believed it.

> Americans and Vietnamese march together, fight together, and die together, and it is hard to get much more involved than that.
>
> David Halberstam, New York *Times,* October 21, 1962

The policy apparently was to keep the American public in the dark:

> Although there are an estimated 10,000 American military men in Vietnam . . . on this and other operations foreign correspondents have been prevented from covering the action close-up. An official news blackout has been imposed by U.S. and Vietnamese officials.
>
> New York *Herald Tribune,* November 23, 1962

In spite of the blackout, the public was learning something of the nature of the U.S. involvement:

> This is a dirty, cruel war, as dirty and as cruel as the war waged by French forces in Algeria which so shocked the American conscience.
>
> *The Nation,* January 19, 1963

15. After Diem

In November 1963, after a period of mounting rioting and unrest, the U.S. Government finally concluded that Diem's usefulness was at an end and it made clear that it could no longer support him in power. Diem was almost at once overthrown and assassinated.

After his death, a few of those who had been unjustly thrown into jail were released, and the full brutality of his regime was permitted to become known. Jean Lacouture, the well-known French correspondent, after interviewing some of these released prisoners, wrote *(Viet-Nam Between Two Truces,* p. 98):

> Hundreds of students of both sexes had been subjected to ill-treatment. Many had been forced to drink soapy water until they had suffered internal damage. At the detention camp in Le Van Quich forty prisoners at a time were thrown into a cell in the hot sun. Others had their nails torn out; still others were blinded.

During Diem's regime tens of thousands were imprisoned, mutilated, and executed. Such was the rule of the "inspired leader fighting for the free world," the "Churchill of Vietnam"!

We need not describe here the hectic efforts made by the U.S. Government after Diem's death to find *someone* who could mount an effective military campaign against the National Liberation Front and through whom it could re-establish control in Saigon. The search for such a man proved fruitless. One regime followed another in quick succession. By January 1965 seven changes of government had taken place; by mid-1965 no fewer than thirteen. As each new leader stepped briefly onto the stage he was hailed by the United States as the "answer" to the problem of Vietnam leadership. Each in turn collapsed and disappeared from sight.

One such leader, General Nguyen Cao Ky, a jet pilot trained by the French at the height of the Algerian crisis, and the commander of the Vietnamese air force, lasted somewhat longer than the rest. He demonstrated his belief in freedom and democracy within a few hours of his attaining power by suppressing a large number of newspapers. Later President Johnson paid Ky the unusual compliment of flying to Honolulu to meet him. There he publicly embraced him, and together they issued a ringing "Declaration of Honolulu" which promised to bring social reforms to south Vietnam. But Ky, like all the others before him, failed to gain the respect and allegiance of his people.

"People ask me who my heroes are. I have only one —Adolf Hitler."
General Ky

The Vietnamese people are not looking for modest, U.S.-sponsored "reforms" but a thoroughgoing clean-up of their political system and a total change in their situation. They want to sweep away once and forever the corruption and self-aggrandizement that has brought their country to the brink of disintegration, and above all they want to rid their country of foreign control. It never dawned on Johnson that his support of Ky in Hawaii was almost a kiss of death, that after arming the detested French regime and sponsoring the merciless dictatorship of Diem, the United States could hardly support *any* leader who would not be suspect and unacceptable.

By this time the majority of the Vietnamese had come to a full realization that for all its protestations and talk of aid and friendship, the United States was not concerned with the well-being of Vietnam but only with its own interests.

16. The Nature of the Vietnam Revolution

The leaders of the United States in south Vietnam have shown a profound inability to understand the nature of revolutionary warfare.

To judge by its actions, the U.S. Government appears to believe that the problem in south Vietnam is primarily a *technical* one.

Given enough military equipment (so the theory goes) any revolution can

> "After 48 hours in South Vietnam Mr. McNamara was tremendously encouraged by developments . . . 'I found nothing but progress and hope for the future' he said."
>
> *N.Y. Times,* May 12, 1962
>
> "The war in Vietnam is going well . . ."
>
> MCNAMARA, January 1963
>
> "The major part of the U.S. military task can be completed by the end of 1965."
>
> MCNAMARA, October 1963
>
> "The U.S. still hopes to withdraw most of its troops from South Vietnam before the end of 1965."
>
> MCNAMARA, February 1964
>
> "We have stopped losing the war."
>
> MCNAMARA, October 1965

be suppressed. The human and political factors, not measurable by computer, are ignored. But Vietnam shows why it is primarily these factors that are the most crucial. To the frustration of the U.S. military theorists, immense superiority in equipment and advanced military expertise have so far not brought about the expected suppression of the liberation forces. Nothing is more revealing than the number of optimistic expectations voiced at the highest levels of the military command which have subsequently been disproved by events. On February 18, 1964, for example, Secretary of Defense McNamara told members of Congress that the U.S. "still hopes to withdraw most of its troops from South Vietnam before the end of 1965." (At the end of 1965 he said in Saigon that "We have stopped losing the war.") On innumerable occasions the U.S. leaders have told the American people that all was going well in south Vietnam—only to be confronted almost immediately with further setbacks.

The inability of the military mind to grasp the nature and the power of a liberation movement is a recurring feature of history. The French, in their attempts to defeat the liberation forces in Vietnam, were just as stubbornly, and wrongly, optimistic as the U.S. Government has shown itself to be today. In fact, some of Johnson's and McNamara's statements could have been written by the French.

Some months before the total defeat of the French at Dien Bien Phu, Deputy René Kuehn was telling the French Parliament:

> Victory *is* possible, certain, and almost immediate if, right away Vietnamese officials will resolutely launch into the necessary political and social reforms and correct their mistakes.
>
> *Journal Officiel,* October 27, 1953

Deputy Raymond Dronne also took a line that was to become familiar in the United States ten years later:

> To speak of negotiations is the surest means of raising the morale of the adversary and of demoralizing our own troops.
>
> *Journal Officiel,* October 23, 1953

The men in Washington have not only shown themselves to be as poor prophets as the French, but they have attempted to convince the American people that the revolutionary movement enjoys little support among the Vietnamese people.

> "There is little evidence," said Mr. Dean Rusk on April 23rd, 1965, "that the Vietcong has any significant popular following in South Vietnam."

The stupendous audacity of such a statement is breathtaking. Rusk asks us to believe that 250,000 U.S. troops, plus 60,000 members of the Seventh Fleet, plus 600,000 troops of the south Vietnamese army, paid for and equipped by the United States, plus the U.S. Air Force and the support of the huge bombing forces stationed in Guam—that this unimaginably vast array of military power is being deployed against an insurgent force of guerrillas who have no real backing of the people!

Secretary Rusk is either deceiving the American people or he is ignorant of what a liberation movement is. In view of his position it is difficult to know which alternative is the more frightening.

He should know that revolutionaries invariably consider the support of the people as essential to their success—and winning the allegiance of the people must always be their *primary objective*. Guerrilla fighting on a large scale such as we are seeing in south Vietnam becomes possible only when the existing government has *morally alienated* itself from the masses. The revolutionary aim is to widen this moral isolation until (as has happened in south Vietnam) the isolation has become irreversible. The lesson that Rusk and his colleagues still need to learn is that the moral isolation of the U.S.–Saigon government has reached the point where no matter *what* promises are made for "social reform," no matter *what* billion-dollar plans for reconstruction the U.S. offers, the people of Vietnam will have none of them. That is why the Declaration of Honolulu brought no acceptance, but merely added contempt for those who made it.

According to W. W. Rostow (now one of the President's closest advisers), a revolutionary movement enjoys one great advantage because "its task is merely to destroy while the government must build and protect what it is building." Again one wonders how a close adviser of the President can become so removed from the realities. What Rostow says contradicts the whole history of liberation movements and flies in the face of reports from every foreign observer who has concerned himself with the nature of the Vietnam revolutionary struggle.

> "Even Premier Ky told this reporter today that the Communists were closer to the people's yearnings for social justice and an independent life than his own government."
>
> James Reston, New York *Times*, September 1, 1965

Far from "merely destroying," accounts from Westerners who have visited the areas under the control of the Liberation Movement indicate that large-scale social reforms are being introduced. Thousands of hectares of land have been distributed to poor peasants; more than 1,500 schools have been opened; village medical services have been started; a national campaign against illiteracy has been launched; and more than fifty-seven newspapers and periodicals are now being published in various areas under N.L.F. control.

It is in the very nature of a revolutionary movement to introduce basic social and political reforms; if it does not, it ceases to be a revolutionary movement. Unless it establishes an administrative apparatus that can begin to meet the aspirations of the people, unless this is an integral part of the liberation movement, the struggle is no more than a form of banditry, which will never receive the support of the people and is doomed to defeat. This is certainly not the story in south Vietnam.

Finally, an enormous effort has been made to persuade the American people that "terror" is one of the chief weapons of the liberation forces and that such support as they can muster among the people is given only reluctantly and by coercion. This, too, flies in the face of reality. Successful guerrilla warfare cannot, as we have said, be conducted without the support of the people, and such support cannot be obtained by threats. Nothing would alienate the masses more quickly than to be under coercion, and such alienation simply has not occurred. How possibly could large contingents of liberation fighters move, without being betrayed, in every direction across the country; how could they bring their forces and weapons almost to the gates of U.S. air bases, or place mortars within three miles of the center of Saigon, without great numbers of people being aware of and covering these movements? How could the guerrilla fighters have developed their superb intelligence system if the people everywhere were not ready and willing to pass on information regarding the movements of the U.S. troops?

The truth is precisely the *reverse* of what the public is being told. President Johnson may be reluctant to state the truth that mass support is being given to the liberation forces. His predecessor was not. "I am convinced," said Kennedy while he was still a Senator, "that American military aid, no matter how extensive, cannot, crush an enemy who . . . *commands the support and sympathy* of the people."

The village chiefs, we are told, are assassinated by the liberation fighters. Or are they killed, one must ask, by the villagers themselves? For who, in the eyes of the Vietnamese, are these chiefs but traitors, the representatives of a government that has sold out to the foreign invader? Senator Russell, chairman of the Armed Services Committee, in a speech in the Senate on March 21, 1966, made the position of these "village chiefs" quite clear:

> We are not able to garrison a locality and then move on to another place. That is the reason that the so-called march-and-destroy tactics are employed. . . . They have not undertaken to hold the ground that they have taken. We have taken some areas two or three times. . . . We turn [an area] over to the South Vietnamese . . . *We appoint the Governor of a village* and give him a half dozen armed villages, and they do not last too long if the Vietcong come back.

In other words, these "village chiefs" are not village chiefs at all but appointees of the U.S. No wonder "they do not last too long"!

As for "terror," it seems to most foreign observers a monstrous absurdity for the Americans to protest the activities of the liberation forces while their own planes drop hundreds of thousands of tons of high explosives upon defenseless villages and burn to death every living being within them. How can the villagers of Vietnam, poor beyond our comprehension of poverty (most of them in their whole lives have not so much as ridden in an automobile)—how can

> Yesterday, within hours of President Johnson's peech, United States bombers carried out more aids on North Vietnam than on any other day this ear. The 'progress' that President Johnson talked bout . . . is towards the destruction of the country, oth North and South."
>
> ditorial, *The Guardian* (London), June 1, 1966

such people resist the napalm and white phosphorous, the bombs and rockets and planes and helicopters, the whole huge arsenal of modern weaponry which is at the disposal of the American army, except by mobilizing the spirit of patriotism of the villagers to the point where they are ready to fight with their bare hands if need be to throw out the invading foreigners? If the Japanese had invaded the United States after Pearl Harbor, would not the American people have done the same? And would they not with equal fury have turned on any traitors within their own country who had thrown in their lot with the invaders?

"Back in 1776 British 'experts' were sure they could beat the ragged colonists. . . . The British had the second best army in the world; the colonists only those ridiculous guerrillas. . . . The British lost because they didn't understand the power of *wars of national liberation.*"

Sidney Lens, *Liberation*, February 1966

The militarily powerful have always looked with disdain at the militarily weak. It was true in the American War of Independence; it is still true today. We have seen how (until Dien Bien Phu) the French colonial officers spoke with contempt of the "Vietminh," calling them *les jaunes,* the yellow ones—yellow in color, yellow in cowardice. And true to form, this is what Under Secretary of State George W. Ball thinks of the liberation forces, published in a State Department publication in 1962 (*Vietnam Free-World Challenge in Southeast Asia,* page 15):

> The guerrillas . . . are poorly trained and equipped and not motivated by deep conviction. Rather, they are merely unsophisticated villagers or peasants who have been conscripted by terror or treachery. In such a case they are likely to have had only rudimentary training in weapon handling and tactics. Their equipment may be makeshift, often just what they can capture or fabricate themselves.

Neil Sheehan, a New York *Times* correspondent in Vietnam, reported that U.S. military men often dismiss the guerrilla fighters as "raggedly little bastards in black pajamas."

Several years and many thousands of lives later, these intimidated, unsophisticated, poorly trained, unmotivated, ill-equipped, raggedly little bastards are still successfully defying the greatest military power the world has ever seen.

17. The U.S. Escalates the War

By early 1965 the situation in south Vietnam was rapidly disintegrating. Morale in Saigon had sunk to a new low. The desertion rate among the government troops reached alarming proportions: at one time, it was reported, 30 percent of inductees were deserting within the first three months.

"Yes, the Americans have bombing planes, jeeps; they can move and fly very fast. But we can be faster than them, because we in south Vietnam are already there."

Huynh Minh—member of the N.L.F. resistance forces

Failure to make headway against the National Liberation Front presented the U.S. Government with a dilemma—whether to admit defeat and leave Vietnam or to break out from the jungles and swamps of south Vietnam. Washington decided that victory would still be possible in the context of a wider war.

U.S. News & World Report on October 12, 1964, said that south Vietnam, in spite of vast U.S. military help and economic aid, was simply falling apart. And Joseph Alsop, writing in the New York *Herald Tribune* December 23, 1964, predicted that "if stern measures are not taken pretty soon . . . the United States is almost certainly doomed to suffer the greatest defeat in American history."

> Against this background of crumbling collapse, U.S. military advisers are insisting that the war must be carried, with American participation and under American direction, across the frontier into North Vietnam.
>
> *Sunday Times* (London), February 23, 1965

One year later Senator Russell was to refer to this period in Congress *(Congressional Record,* March 21, 1966):

> I do not believe the South Vietnamese forces would have lasted another month because they were on the verge of disintegration.

To bomb north Vietnam was clearly an act of military desperation—but one that had to have a pretext. The pretext? "To stop the weapons from the north reaching the 'Vietcong.'" It was the birth of the "aggression from the north" theory.

The feverish debate as to whether or not to bomb north Vietnam drowned out the realities:

> The guerrillas are obviously not being reinforced or supplied systematically from North Vietnam, China, or any other place. They depend primarily on what they can capture.
>
> General Paul D. Harkins, Head of U.S. Operations in south Vietnam, March 6, 1963

> No capture of North Vietnamese in the South has come to light.
>
> David Halberstam, New York *Times,* March 6, 1964

> There is not one shred of credible evidence that the bulk of munitions used by the Vietcong originate in the north. At the outset, the Vietcong used crude homemade weapons, but the bulk of their arms now are captured or otherwise acquired from the woefully inept defenders of South Vietnam.
>
> New York *World-Telegram,* January 4, 1965

"Reprisal raids . . . lead us to think of the retaliation of the Nazis during World War II when they killed ten members of the French resistance whenever a German soldier was killed."

Congressman Robert Nix (Pa.), March 16, 1965

But the decision to escalate the war to north Vietnam had already been taken and, in fact, had already begun the previous summer.

On the night of August 4 the American destroyer *Maddox,* which had been in action two days earlier against three north Vietnamese torpedo boats, signaled that she and her sister ship were "being attacked by communist naval vessels." The accounts issued by the U.S. Government were obscure and contradictory, and many observers around the world remain to this day uncertain whether these ships were really attacked.

Within a few hours, however, President Johnson told the American people on TV that reprisal raids on north Vietnam had been ordered and that the planes were already on their way. Two massive air attacks were staged which the U.S. claimed destroyed half of north Vietnam's naval strength, and oil storage depots.

The long-debated "escalation" had begun. Now, without a shred of moral or legal justification, the war was no longer directed against a frustratingly effective enemy in the south but against the north, which was administered by a government that was an ally of China and of the Soviet Union.

To justify the bombing of north Vietnam it became necessary to convince the American people that the war in the south was not a liberation struggle against the U.S. forces but an "invasion," a "war of aggression," against the south launched and controlled from Hanoi. This was not easy. As the New York *Times* put it in a stinging editorial (April 30, 1965):

> For months during the campaign against Senator Goldwater, the Administration line was that the war in South Vietnam was substantially self-sustaining and had to be won there. Almost overnight, when the bombing of North Vietnam began, information was produced to prove that "aggression from the North" . . . is the key to everything. . . . Nor is Washington's credibility increased by the President's insistence at the very time that we widen the war, that he is against any "wider war" and has not changed his policy.

On February 27, 1965, the State Department issued a White Paper which it was hoped would sound convincing. It did not sound convincing at all. In attempting to prove how massive the aid was that was allegedly pouring down from north Vietnam, the White Paper succeeded only in indicating how *little* aid was being sent. If Hanoi had indeed been carrying on an "elaborate program" of arming the guerrillas, it was odd (as critics of the White Paper were quick to point out) that of 15,100 weapons captured from the guerrilla forces in the previous three years only 179 were not manufactured in Western countries—and these could have been bought commercially almost anywhere in the world.

"Your attempt now to pin the whole blame on the government of North Vietnam deceives no one except those whose wishful thinking originally committed us to our high-handed intervention; the same set of agencies and intelligencies that inveigled us into the Bay of Pigs disaster."

Lewis Mumford in an open letter to President Johnson

A great deal of talk has taken place about the aid being sent to the liberation forces from the north, but there has been very little hard evidence. Senator Wayne Morse has repeatedly asked Administration witnesses to produce incontrovertible proof of the alleged "aggression." He said in the Senate on July 24 1965:

> No one in the U.S. Government has been able, to this hour, to lay any evidence before the Committee on Foreign Relations that he has been able to find military forces of North Vietnam or China in South Vietnam.

But "dramatic new proof" *was* presented by the White Paper of "large shipments of arms" that were reaching the liberation forces by sea. This "dramatic proof" turned out to be the capture of a wooden junk of 100 tons carrying a small amount of weapons that again could have been bought from surplus-stock agencies anywhere in the world. An Associated Press report from Saigon put this capture in its right perspective:

> About 12,000 vessels are searched *each month* . . . but [until this single capture] no significant amounts of incriminating goods or weapons ever have been found.

Rarely has any official paper received such scathing attacks as this White Paper, and it deserved them. It was selective in the information it gave and what it withheld; it studiously refused to mention any evidence that would indicate south Vietnam was engaged in a liberation struggle; it carefully avoided any mention of the elections promised under the Geneva Agreements or the refusal of the U.S.-Diem government to hold them. The notorious concentration camps, which the U.S. chose to call "strategic hamlets," were described in the White Paper as "designed to improve the peasant's livelihood." The appalling unemployment and destitution of the people in south Vietnam was referred to in the White Paper as Diem's "economic miracle."

> We are asked to believe [wrote I. F. Stone in a devastating analysis of the White Paper] that for the first time in history a guerrilla war spread not because the people were discontented but because their lot was improving!
>
> *I. F. Stone's Weekly,* March 8, 1965

The White Paper was embarrassing even to staunch supporters of Administration policy. It is little wonder that it was quickly buried and that almost nothing is heard of it now.

Thirteen months later—during all of which time the U.S. Government was claiming that Hanoi had been sending forces south at "an increasing rate"—Senator Clark revealed *(Congressional Record,* March 21, 1966) that Secretary McNamara had testified that of the 235,000 enemy effectives in south Vietnam, only 15,000 were north Vietnamese regulars, or something under 6.5 percent—this after thirteen months of "heavy infiltration."

In the same Senate debate, Senator Russell, chairman of the Armed Services Committee, added several additional interesting admissions. He said that there are no Chinese or Russians fighting in south Vietnam, and that

> . . . the South Vietnamese are fighting under almost incredible odds, not having any air force to protect them, but they are fighting and fighting very bravely . . . I think that a good deal of the Vietcong affiliation is a legacy from the war against the French where Ho Chi Minh was the leader of what they believed, with considerable reason, was a call of liberation.
>
> Of course we supported the efforts of the French with substantial funds . . . I do not know how much the Vietcong support is because of a firm belief in communism as a system of government . . . I believe a greater part of it is personal

"The day-to-day communiques give the impression that we win almost every encounter, but we somehow merely advance deeper into the bog."

James Reston, New York *Times,* November 14, 1965

affection, respect and admiration for and belief in Ho Chi Minh, rather than any set of political principles.

The publication of the White Paper on February 27, 1965, was timed to precede by a few days a further intensification of the bombing war against north Vietnam. On March 2, the U.S. Air Force began systematic round-the-clock bombardment. There was no longer any attempt to justify these attacks as "reprisals":

> . . . the Americans began to consider themselves entitled to hit the North at their discretion. The North was guilty because it was communist, because it was a neighbor and accomplice of a people on whose territory armed forces of the United States suffered cruel disappointments, because it did not close its doors to its compatriots from the South who were engaged in combat against the greatest power in the world.
>
> Jean Lacouture, *Viet-Nam Between Two Truces,* p. 265

The United States put forward three objectives which, it was hoped, the bombing of north Vietnam would accomplish: force the north Vietnamese to end their support of the National Liberation Front; force Hanoi to negotiate, and increase the fighting morale of the Saigon Government.

It failed in all three.

> After a year of increasing escalation, the area controlled by the Viet Cong is larger today than it was a year ago, and the North Vietnamese have replied to the bombing not by ceasing to intervene in South Vietnam, but by doing what it was plain that they would do if we bombed them, by sending in more and more of their trained troops.
>
> Walter Lippmann, San Francisco *Chronicle,* January 2, 1966

Thus, after a year of heavy bombing (there were over 20,000 bombing sorties over north Vietnam in the first ten months in 1965—about 65 a day) north Vietnam was less inclined than ever to capitulate; the number of troops and equipment coming from the north have been officially stated in Washington to be significantly *higher* than before the bombing began; and the fighting morale in the south was no better than before.

A concrete indication of improvement in the morale of the south Vietnamese forces would be a drop in the rate of desertions. A New York *Times* dispatch from Saigon on February 24, 1966, reported that the number of deserters had risen steadily during 1965. By the year's end 113,000 troops had deserted. (The number of desertions in 1964 was estimated as 72,000.) In 1966 the desertion rate rose still further and McNamara was forced to admit on May 11, 1966, that 12,000 were deserting *every month*.

The extent of corruption is another indication of morale. The San Francisco *Chronicle* on October 31, 1965, reported that high-ranking Vietnamese officials

In early 1966 the wife of an American aid official in south Vietnam sent home $36,000 within six months to be deposited to her account in the United States. The Government said it would "investigate."

readily admitted that corruption was more widespread than at any time since the overthrow of Diem. On February 25, 1966, the same paper ran an article by Stanley Karnow describing how "about everybody's in on graft in Saigon," and that sideline activities are so widespread and so profitable "that most Vietnamese civil servants can find only a little time to handle their formal functions." One of Diem's successors, General Khanh, publicly boasted that he had put aside $10 million in foreign banks (New York *Herald Tribune,* February 3, 1964).

> At some point, the President and his advisers are going to have to ask themselves why everything goes wrong . . . why over the years all our hopes have been dashed and one plan after another has failed . . . It is, I believe, that we have set ourselves a task, which, like squaring the circle or perpetual motion or living 200 years, is impossible to do. It is an impossible task for the United States to reach across the Pacific Ocean and . . . by force of American arms to assure a weak country that it will be non-Communist.
>
> Walter Lippmann, *Newsweek,* July 19, 1965

But the United States Government after twelve years of failure continues to try.

> Escalation has its own perverse logic; the less effective it proves, the more insistent becomes the demands to do more and more.
>
> New York *Times,* July 22, 1965

18. What Kind of War is Going on in Vietnam?

"President Johnson is on the verge of making the kind of ruinous historical mistake which . . . Hitler made when he attacked Russia."
Walter Lippmann, January 4, 1966

This is the key question.

The United States still insists—against all available evidence and contrary to reports by all foreign observers—that what is going on is "aggression from the north"; that the National Liberation Front was initiated and is controlled by Hanoi. The U.S. role in Vietnam, it is said, is merely to give a helping hand to the south, which is the victim of this aggression. The whole public justification for U.S. intervention in south Vietnam, and for the bombing of north Vietnam, rests on this case and enormous efforts have been made to make the case sound plausible. Spokesmen for the U.S. Government have conceded that if, indeed, the struggle in Vietnam is a civil war, the U.S. has no right whatever to be there. "If it was an indigenous rebellion," said George W. Ball, Under Secretary of State (Washington *Post,* February 6, 1966), "the United States would have no business taking sides in the conflict and helping one side to defeat the other by force of arms."

Those who oppose U.S. intervention in Vietnam realize the grotesque absurdity of the U.S. "aggression from the north" theory. They know that the facts simply do not support it. Many of them see this war as a struggle that began as a legitimate revolt against a repressive and cruel regime, and that has, they believe, since developed into a full-fledged civil war.

> It was not North Vietnam, or even local Communists, but Ngo Dinh Diem who finally drove the whole countryside into rebellion.
>
> Edgar Snow, *The Other Side of the River,* p. 701

And Professor Hans J. Morgenthau, one-time adviser to the State Department and a strong critic of U.S. policies in Vietnam, referred to the struggle as a civil war when he wrote:

> The United States has decided to change the character of the war by unilateral declaration from a South Vietnamese civil war to a war of "foreign aggression."
>
> *New York Times Magazine,* April 18, 1965, p. 86

"The mistake of the Americans is to think that the Vietnamese affair is simply a phase of the struggle between the Communist and capitalist worlds and to believe that if it were not for a Machiavellian plot by China, nothing would happen in Vietnam. But today the rebellion in Vietnam is popular. North Vietnam and China support it, but it has a life of its own. Neither Hanoi nor Peking commands the Vietcong."
Former French Premier Edgar Faure, *Figaro,* February 17, 1965

However, when the historic sequence of events is examined, it will be seen that the struggle in Vietnam is no more a "civil war" than it is a war against "aggression from the north."

When the French were in occupation of what is now Vietnam, though a number of Vietnamese supported the French and acted as their agents, the Vietnamese resistance against the French was never considered a "civil war." Nor could the struggle against the Japanese occupation conceivably be called a "civil war," though, again, some Vietnamese threw their lot in with the invading forces. The renewed war of resistance against the French after World War II was never termed a "civil war." When the U.S. took over from the French, whom they had armed and financed, the nature of the war was not in any way altered. It did not become a "civil war" because it was now the United States and not France which became the occupying power.

History has shown that a foreign occupying force can *always* secure the support of some of the local population. In the American Revolution 150,000 Americans sided with the British. Did this make the revolution a "civil war"? Even Hitler was supported by a puppet French government, but this did not in any sense make the struggle of the French resistance against the Germans a "civil war."

The presence in Vietnam of a local, U.S. supported, U.S. financed, U.S. armed regime cannot obscure the central fact that the main objective of the liberation struggle, from the beginning and at every stage since, has been *the removal of foreign military force.*

It would probably come as a painful surprise to many Americans to realize how universally the war in Vietnam is viewed not as a "complex issue" but as

> "The Asians with whom I've talked see a rich, powerful, predominantly white nation trying to impose its will on Southeast Asia by using its overwhelming military power. They see us as a bully."
>
> Rev. Dr. Eugene Carson Blake, General Secretary, World Council of Churches

a simple and blatant act of aggression by the United States. While the U.S. Government issues its comforting formulas about "fulfilling our commitments" and "resisting aggression from the north" many of the closest friends of the United States are voicing their sense of moral outrage at this country's actions in Vietnam.

A large number of the most respected citizens of Canada in a widely published statement have said bluntly: "The United States has *invaded South Vietnam* with 250,000 troops" (Ottawa *Citizen,* March 25, 1966). In the Canadian Parliament, conservative members have condemned U.S. actions as (in the words of one of them) *"a war of terrorism* against the people." Throughout Europe, although certain allied governments may voice formal support of the U.S., leading public figures are denouncing United States actions in Vietnam as *aggression*— morally, politically, and militarily unjustifiable.

And not only in Europe. In 1965 the staunchly pro-United States government of Japan sent one of their most experienced diplomats, Shunichi Matsumoto, to Vietnam to survey the situation. His report infuriated official Washington. Matsumoto did not believe that the National Liberation Front was predominantly a "Communist movement"; he did not think the conflict could be won by military means; he thought the insurgent forces could be "called a movement somewhat similar to the resistance of the French underground during World War II"—in other words, *a patriotic resistance against a foreign invader.*

It was to wage a struggle against a foreign-appointed regime that the National Liberation Front of south Vietnam was formed in the first place. There is no war as such between south and north Vietnam precisely because the struggle is neither the result of "aggression from the north" nor a "civil war," but a war against foreign military invasion. To call it a "civil war" is as misleading as to call it "aggression from the north." It remains—despite every effort to conceal it—*essentially a war by the Vietnamese people against the military invasion of their country by the United States.*

There are still some, perhaps, who continue to delude themselves that the war in Vietnam is a "struggle between communism and democracy." On May 24, 1966, Secretary-General U Thant said that such a concept was not relevant to the situation:

> Twenty years of outside intervention and the pressure of foreign armies have so profoundly affected Vietnamese political life that it seems illusory to represent it as a mere contest between communism and liberal democracy.
>
> Indeed recent events have shown that the passion for national identity, perhaps one should say national survival, is the only ideology that may be left to a growing number of Vietnamese . . . what is really at stake . . . is the survival of the country itself.

The opposition to U.S. policies in Vietnam by no means stems only from those affiliated with or sympathetic to the Left. No more damning denunciation has been issued than the following editorial in a Catholic review *(Frères du Monde)* published by the Franciscan Order in France (translated and reprinted by the *Gazette and Daily,* York, Pennsylvania, on October 25, 1965):

USA: A SYSTEM WHICH NOURISHES ITSELF BY MEANS OF WAR

. . . In Vietnam, peace is not a football game between two equal teams. On one side, there is an aggressor, the USA, and on the other, a people who are continually being oppressed, bombed, and decimated.

If you do not see the matter in this light, it is because you have admitted that anti-communism is an end that justifies all means, including torture, napalm, and dozens of daily bombardments against North Vietnam. It is because you have accepted the validity of the crusade which is leading the so-called "free world" to intervene wherever its hegemony seems threatened by the revolt of poor peoples. . .

This is where we now are. It is the United States that is killing, burning, and terrorizing . . .

It is the USA which implacably practices the dangerous policy of "escalation" . . . It is the USA which daily is menacing world peace . . .

Such a posture must be denounced. We refuse any longer to be the dupes of an American imperialism which, under the pretext of defending "human values," is doing nothing except assuring its own privileged position in the underdeveloped world; and we say that if a regime is reduced to such strategies and to such crimes in order to preserve itself, then it is a regime which is rotten to the core.

We hold no necessary grudge against the USA, but we say "no" to a system which nourishes itself by means of war, which orients itself toward war and profits handsomely from it. It is imperative that the responsibility for all this be clearly fixed . . .

It is they, and not the Vietnamese patriots, who are causing the killing and suffering—all for a "free and independent South Vietnam."

The matter would be very clear to all of us if the victims were not degraded in our eyes by their communist affiliations. For us, the red star has been enough to lead us to dehumanize our fellow men and to consign some of them to the limbo of pernicious beasts which must be crushed at any price. . . .

Whether we like it or not, the Vietnamese do not desire our way of life; communist or non-communist, they reject our "dirty war." Before being communists, they are above all men who have had enough of western colonialism. It is a revolt —a continuing revolt—to gain true liberty that the USA is attempting to crush in Vietnam, as in Santo Domingo. It is nothing else than this; and the great crime of the USA is the attempt to make us all believe in a crusade for "freedom."

The facts are plain. This war was begun by armed American aggression aimed at perpetuating the unnatural and unintended division of Vietnam into North and South, in full violation of the Geneva Accords of 1954. In complementary man

> "There can be no reasoning with incendiary bombs."
> President Roosevelt, rejecting the German offer of "discussions" after the fall of France, 1940

ner the Americans and the puppet Diem refused to permit the free elections called for by the Geneva Accords; the reason is, as everyone knows . . . that Ho Chi Minh would have won those elections easily.

"The building of the base at Camranh Bay alone represents so huge a commitment that few people in South Vietnam seem to imagine it would be abandoned if the Vietcong or Hanoi suddenly sued for peace."

Editorial, *The Guardian* (London), June 1, 1966

Whether communist or not, Ho is a symbol of the struggle of underdeveloped nations to determine their own destiny. But the USA has solemnly decided to crush this revolution and to transform South Vietnam into an American military base, a "bastion of the free world" which could be used to carry the war to China. If the Vietnamese people stand in the way, they are to be suppressed and, if need be, exterminated.

Of course, we have newer excuses for all this: "aggression from the North" and "Vietcong terrorism." The first is largely a myth which assumes even more grotesque forms in reading the American "white papers" themselves; the second is a distortion of history, as if terrorism has not been, for the weak and oppressed, the only means to protect themselves and make themselves heard—as if, above all, the weapons of the rich and powerful country (napalm, phosphorous and bombs) distinguish more finely between military and civilian and do not have effects immeasurably more atrocious. . . .

These crimes are deliberately repeated by U.S. air and naval forces against North Vietnam by day and night bombings of peaceful villages, without sparing hospitals, schools, markets, churches, power stations, and, recently, a large leprosarium with red crosses painted clearly on its roofs. No matter; the small, poor, virtually defenseless state of North Vietnam must be systematically destroyed.

We shall not get out of this by crying for peace, by praying for peace, or by hoping for a peaceful compromise of the wolf and the sheep. In Vietnam, peace can come only with the liberation of the entire Vietnamese people. In the world, peace can come only through an end to the Cold War and the "anti-communist" disease.

19. What Do the Vietnamese Want?

The National Liberation Front has stated that it would enter into discussions with the U.S. only on the basis of the full acceptance of its ten-point program.

This, the spokesmen for the United States have always flatly rejected. "To accept the N.L.F. program," they say, "would be tantamount to a U.S. defeat."

How many have read the program that so horrifies the United States Government? For the record and without comment we set out a summary of this program here:

SUMMARY OF THE TEN-POINT PROGRAM OF THE NATIONAL LIBERATION FRONT OF SOUTH VIETNAM

(Announced December 20, 1960)

1. To replace the present disguised colonial regime and form a national democratic coalition government including representatives of all strata of the people, of all nationalities, political parties, and religious communities.

2. To bring into being a broad and progressive democracy, to promulgate all democratic freedoms: freedom of expression, of the press, of assembly, of association, of trade unions, of movements. A guarantee of freedom of belief with no discrimination against any religion; and freedom of action to all patriotic political parties and mass organizations irrespective of political tendency.
3. To build an independent national economy, beneficial to the nation and the people; to improve the people's living conditions. Help industrialists and tradespeople to rehabilitate and develop industry both large and small. Apply a rational and equitable tax system; organize social security—with jobs for the unemployed, protection of orphans, the aged, and the disabled.
4. To advance agriculture through reduction in land rents; by means of negotiations to purchase from landowners at equitable prices all land held by them in excess of a given area and distribute it to landless and poor peasants free of charge and without conditions.
5. To develop a national democratic system of education available to all and to further Vietnamese culture. To wipe out illiteracy and expand universities and vocational schools. Develop science and technology and national literature and art; encourage and help intellectuals and cultural workers to develop their abilities. To develop medical services to protect the people's health.
6. To build a national army to defend the Fatherland; to abolish all foreign military bases.
7. To guarantee equality among the various nationalities and between men and women; to protect the legitimate rights of foreigners resident in Vietnam.
8. To pursue a foreign policy of peace and neutrality.
9. To re-establish normal relations between the two zones of Vietnam and advance toward the peaceful reunification of the Fatherland on the basis of negotiations; and pending reunification ensure for the people of both zones freedom of movement and the right to exchange visits and correspondence and to do nothing that might cause division between them.
10. To oppose aggressive war and actively to defend world peace. To oppose war propaganda; to demand general disarmament and the prohibition of nuclear weapons and the use of atomic energy for peaceful purposes.

"My solution? Tell the Vietnamese they've got to draw in their horns and stop aggression or we're going to bomb them back into the Stone Age."
General Curtis Le May

Again for the record we also include here:

FOUR POINTS OF THE DEMOCRATIC REPUBLIC OF VIETNAM

(Announced in a report made to the National Assembly in Hanoi on April 8 1965)

1. Recognition of the basic national rights of the Vietnamese people: peace, independence, sovereignty, unity, and territorial integrity. According to the Geneva Agreements, the U.S. Government must withdraw from South Vietnam all U.S. troops, military personnel and weapons of all kinds, dismantle all U.S. military bases there, cancel its "military alliance" with South Vietnam. It must end its policy of intervention and aggression in South Vietnam. According to the Geneva

Agreements, the U.S. Government must stop its acts of war against North Vietnam, end definitely all encroachments on the territory and sovereignty of the Democratic Republic of Vietnam.

2. Pending the peaceful reunification of Vietnam, while Vietnam is still temporarily divided into two zones, the military provisions of the 1954 Geneva Agreements on Vietnam must be strictly respected: the two zones must refrain from joining any military alliance with foreign countries, there must be no foreign military bases, troops, and military personnel in their respective territory.
3. The affairs of South Vietnam must be settled by the South Vietnamese people themselves, in accordance with the program of the South Vietnam National Liberation Front, without any foreign interference.
4. The peaceful reunification of Vietnam is to be settled by the Vietnamese people in both zones, without any foreign interference.

"I hope Red China gives us an excuse to knock the chip off its shoulder."
Barry Goldwater

To clarify their position further the following statement was added:

The Government of the Democratic Republic of Vietnam is of the view that the above-expounded stand is the basis for the soundest political settlement of the Vietnam problem. If this basis is recognized, favorable conditions will be created for the peaceful settlement of the Vietnam problem.

It is the acceptance of these programs which spokesmen for the U.S. Government have declared would be "tantamount to a defeat"!

20. The Art of Double-talk

"When I use a word," Humpty Dumpty said in rather a scornful tone, "it means just what I choose it to mean, neither more nor less."

"The question is," said Alice, "whether you *can* make words mean so many different things."

"The question is," said Humpty Dumpty, "who is to be master, that's all."

Alice in Wonderland

The Vietnam war provides a rich hunting ground for any scholar who wishes to learn the methods a government employs to confuse its own people. Sometimes the double-talk is not noticed, or only by a few. If too many people notice it, it is called "the crisis of credibility." After several years of evasion, secrecy, suppression, "managed news," distortion of facts, and downright lying, the American people can no longer take *any* statement of their government on its face value—and this has become especially true regarding statements about the war in Vietnam. Belief in the truthfulness of the U.S. Government is one of the major casualties of this war.

Let us examine a few examples.

ITEM On April 6, 1964, Adlai Stevenson, representing the United States at the United Nations, declared:

> My government has repeatedly expressed its emphatic disapproval of provocative acts and *retaliatory raids* wherever they occur and by whomever committed.

BUT

On February 7, 1965, President Johnson issued the following statement:

> United States . . . air elements were directed to launch *retaliatory attacks* against barracks and staging areas of North Vietnam.

ITEM On March 3, 1966, Robert S. McNamara, in all solemnity, told the Senate Foreign Relations Committee that "only 109 South Vietnamese civilians have been killed as a result of U.S. military action in the last seven months" (Cleveland *Press,* March 5, 1966). ("Some of the Senators," the newspaper reported, "were openly incredulous of McNamara's statistics.") The same figure was released two weeks later by Assistant Secretary of Defense John T. McNaughton. McNaughton said that in January and February only six civilians were killed.

BUT

On January 5, 1966, Major General James W. Humphreys, head of the U.S. medical aid program in Vietnam, told a press conference in Washington that the war was causing more casualties to civilians than to the military.

On March 17, 1966, Congressman Clement J. Zablocki made public a report which indicated that some operations have resulted in six civilian casualties to one Vietcong. On the basis of Defense Department figures of Vietcong killed, there were 14,000 civilians killed in January and February—not six.

(As a contrast to Secretary McNamara's comforting statistics, one might compare the figures issued a year earlier by the N.L.F. on March 22, 1965:

—nearly 170,000 civilians killed
—nearly 800,000 wounded or disabled by torture
—tens of thousands of women raped
—over five million people herded into "strategic hamlets," "re-settlement areas," etc.)

ITEM The 1961 U.S. Government Blue Book on Vietnam said that the basic pattern of "Vietcong activity" was "not new, of course," the same methods having been used "in Malaya, in Greece, in the Philippines, in Cuba, and in Laos."

BUT

The 1965 White Paper, which attempted to prove the "aggression from the north" theory, declares the conflict "a new brand of aggression . . . *not* another

Greece . . . *not* another Malaya . . . *not* another Philippines . . . Above all . . . *not* a spontaneous and local rebellion against the established government" (italics in original).

ITEM On January 12, 1966, President Johnson said:

> We seek neither territory nor bases, economic domination or military alliance in Vietnam.

BUT

Marquis Childs in his column one month later wrote:

> So massive is the commitment to this [Pacific] empire that the Vietnam war is seen as only one phase . . . of the thrust of American power . . . But it is in the thrust of the far-flung construction effort that the *permanence* of the Pacific empire is evident. Hundreds of millions of dollars are going . . . to build whole new harbors, docks, large military installations . . . Camranh Bay is a construction rivalling anything in America. New jet airstrips cover thousands of acres . . . *the lasting nature of this Pacific endeavor becomes clear.*
>
> Washington *Post*, February 14, 1966

ITEM On February 18, 1964, McNamara told members of Congress that there were about 15,000 U.S. troops in south Vietnam and that the government hoped to bring most of them home by the end of 1964. He said:

> I don't believe that we as a nation should assume the primary responsibility for the war in South Vietnam . . . A counter guerrilla war can only be won by the Vietnamese themselves.

BUT

By April 20, 1966, the number of U.S. troops in south Vietnam had increased to 260,000 and, it was announced, would be increased still further. The 600,000 troops of the Saigon regime are entirely equipped and financed by the United States. Even the south Vietnam *non*-military budget is 75 percent paid for by the U.S. Military activities are now initiated and conducted without reference to the Saigon regime.

If the U.S. is not taking the "primary responsibility" for the war, *who is?*

ITEM On August 31, 1964, the State Department issued this bulletin:

> Some . . . are eager to enlarge the conflict. They call upon us to supply American boys to do the job that Asian boys should do. They ask us to take reckless action which might risk the lives of millions . . . such action would offer no solution at all to the real problem of Viet Nam.

BUT

Within six months the bombing of north Vietnam on a round-the-clock basis had begun. By mid-1966 it was expected that before the end of the year the

U.S. would "supply" 400,000 American boys presumably "to do the job that Asian boys should do."

ITEM On May 11, 1966, President Johnson said:

"We have used our power in Vietnam with great restraint."

BUT

The next day it was revealed that the expenditure on artillery and mortar shells and machine gun and rifle bullets *alone* was $7 million a day (San Francisco *Chronicle,* May 12, 1966).

On April 20, 1966, McNamara told the Senate Foreign Relations Committee that the U.S. was planning to drop 638,000 tons of bombs in Vietnam during 1966—half the total tonnage the U.S. used against the Nazi forces in Europe and Africa *in all of World War II.*

Newsweek, on October 18, 1965, reported that the U.S. Air Force flew no fewer than 26,858 sorties against Vietnam in *a single week.*

ITEM "Candor" said President Johnson on July 13, 1965, "compels me to tell you that there has not been the slightest indication that the other side is interested in negotiation or in unconditional discussions, although the United States has made some dozen separate attempts to bring that about."

BUT

On November 16, 1965, the New York *Times* printed the following:

The State Department confirmed today a report that a year ago the United States had rejected an offer by North Vietnam to have representatives of the two nations meet in Rangoon, Burma to discuss terms for ending hostilities.

In actual fact the U.S. had rejected *no fewer than seven efforts* to negotiate an end to the war. In the fall of 1963 Secretary Rusk turned down a French proposal; in July 1964 the U.S. rejected proposals put forward by U Thant; in December 1964 Ho Chi Minh notified France of his readiness to have discussions with the U.S., but the U.S. scornfully rejected this; in early February 1965 President de Gaulle requested a reconvening of the Geneva Conference—also rejected by the U.S.; on February 24, 1965, the Soviet Union pressed for the reconvening of the Geneva Conference; at the same time U Thant suggested possible preliminary discussions and an informal seven-power conference—both proposals were rejected by the U.S.

ITEM On June 2, 1964, President Johnson said:

America keeps her word . . . In the case of Vietnam our commitment today is just the same as the commitment made by President Eisenhower in 1954.

On August 14, 1965, Dean Rusk referred to the "bilateral arrangements" made by President Eisenhower which committed the U.S. to send troops to Vietnam.

BUT

Eisenhower says he made no such commitment. He is right. The "bilateral arrangements" referred to are supposedly contained in a letter sent by President Eisenhower to Diem on October 23, 1954. This letter is nothing more than a highly tentative, conditional statement of hopes. It contains no "commitment," nothing that could conceivably "obligate" the United States to send a quarter of a million troops and a vast arsenal of equipment to fight the Vietnamese.

ITEM On February 18, 1966, Secretary of State Dean Rusk, no longer able to rely on the Eisenhower letter, produced another "commitment" to justify the war in Vietnam. On that day, in a prepared statement, he told the Senate Foreign Relations Committee that the U.S. was fighting in Vietnam because of the Southeast Asia Treaty Organization (SEATO):

> "It is this fundamental SEATO obligation," he said, "that has from the outset guided our actions in South Vietnam."

BUT

There never was any obligation under SEATO to send troops anywhere. John Foster Dulles, who negotiated the treaty for the U.S. on November 11, 1954, was questioned by the Senate Foreign Relations Committee about U.S. obligations under the SEATO Treaty.

Senator Green asked Mr. Dulles whether the U.S. would be obliged to help put down a revolutionary movement in Vietnam.

Mr. Dulles said:

> No. If there is a revolutionary movement in Vietnam . . . we have no undertaking to put it down; all we have is an undertaking to consult together as to what to do about it.

On February 1, 1955, Senator Smith, a member of the U.S. delegation that negotiated the SEATO Treaty, explained on the floor of the Senate that some nations had hoped:

> to establish an organization modeled on the lines of NATO. . . . Such an organization might have required the commitment of American ground forces to the Asian mainland. We carefully avoided any possible implication regarding an arrangement of that kind.

* * *

Humpty Dumpty is right—he can make words mean what he wants them to mean. From these few examples (and there are hundreds more) we learn that the United States at the U.N. is emphatically against retaliatory raids but that they are fine in Vietnam; that McNamara's computers don't work so well when they are set to counting the civilian dead; that plans to "withdraw troops" mean that more are to be sent; that when the President of the United States begins to talk "with all candor" you had better read the small print; that writers of official pronouncements in Washington rely on people having short memories; and that the U.S. is in this war to honor "commitments" that it never made.

Wrote columnist Richard Starnes in the New York *World-Telegram:*

> Never in the long, squalid history of governments' conditioning people for war has so much rubbish, half-truth, dissembling, falsehood and righteous paltering been heard.

"The question is," said Humpty Dumpty, "who is to be master—that's all."

21. Prelude to Genocide ?

> The following acts, or any of them, are crimes coming within the jurisdiction of the Tribunal for which there shall be individual responsibility:
>
> . . . ill-treatment . . . of civilian population . . . murder or ill-treatment of prisoners of war . . . wanton destruction of cities, towns or villages . . .
> . . . inhumane acts committed against any civilian population.
>
> Charter of the International Military Tribunal
> (Nuremberg Trials)

The mounting fury of the richest and most powerful country is today being directed against one of the smallest and poorest countries in the world. All over the world people are watching with numb horror the sheer brutality of the war that the United States is waging in Vietnam. What, even her best friends are asking, is happening to the American people we once respected?

The evidence is overwhelming and undeniable. No one now even attempts to deny it. Torture, the shooting of prisoners, the use of napalm and phosphorous against civilians, the burning of defenseless villages—all these are now matters of public record:

> "Our people suffered under the French," one veteran of Dien Bien Phu told this writer in Hanoi, "we suffered terribly, terribly. . ." He hesitated and then went on, "But you must know that it was as nothing compared to the suffering inflicted on us today by the Americans."

We do not need to rely on Vietnamese accounts of corroboration in order to be convinced that the United States is engaging in the dirtiest war in its history.

The job of fighting this war falls more heavily on the poor and less educated than on the wealthy and better educated. For the period ending June 1965 16.3 percent of all men drafted were Negro though they represent only 11 percent of the population. Few Negroes attain officer rank (3.5 percent Army; 0.3 percent Air Force; 1.5 percent Navy).

We can turn to the reports of experienced correspondents in the pages of the most responsible newspapers published in the United States.

> Anyone who has spent much time with Government units in the field has seen the heads of prisoners held under water and bayonet blades pressed against their throats. . . . In more extreme cases victims have had bamboo slivers run under their fingernails or wires from a field telephone connected to arms, nipples or testicles.
>
> *New York Times Magazine,* November 28, 1965

> Other techniques, usually designed to force onlooking prisoners to talk, involve cutting off the fingers, ears, fingernails or sexual organs of another prisoner. Sometimes a string of ears decorates the wall of a government military installation.
>
> New York *Herald Tribune,* April 25, 1965

Malcolm Browne, the A.P. correspondent who won a Pulitzer Prize for his reporting of the war, gives some vivid accounts of what goes on in his book *The New Face of War:*

> Many a news correspondent or U.S. Army military adviser has seen the hands whacked off prisoners with machetes. Prisoners are sometimes castrated or blinded.
>
> In more than one case a Viet Cong suspect has been towed after interrogation behind an armored personnel carrier across the rice fields. This always results in death in one of its most painful forms. (p. 116)

Beverly Deepe, a New York *Herald Tribune* correspondent, reports another "interrogation":

> . . . two Viet Cong prisoners were interrogated on an airplane flying toward Saigon. The first refused to answer questions and was thrown out of the airplane at 3,000 feet. The second immediately answered all the questions. But he, too, was thrown out.
>
> New York *Herald Tribune,* April 25, 1965

This is not an isolated case.

> One American helicopter crewman returned to his base in the central highlands last week without a fierce young prisoner entrusted to him. He told friends that he had become infuriated by the youth and had pushed him out of the helicopter at about 1,000 feet.
>
> Jack Langguth, New York *Times,* July 7, 1965

The United States is a signatory to the 1949 Geneva Convention governing the treatment of prisoners. Article 17 states, "No physical or mental torture, nor any other form of coercion, may be inflicted on prisoners of war to secure from them information of any kind whatever." The New York *Times* on December 1, 1965, reported that the "'International Committee of the Red Cross in Geneva . . . complained again that the United States was violating an international accord on the treatment of prisoners."

Earlier, Hans Henle, a former executive of the Information Service of the International Committee of the Red Cross in Geneva, said:

> The Viet Cong fighters are as protected by the Geneva Conventions as the American G.I.'s are. Dramatic protests against violations of the Geneva Conventions should have been made when the first Viet Cong prisoners were shot, when they were tortured, when the American army started to destroy Viet Cong hospitals and to cut off medical supplies. . . . It is utterly hypocritical to condone wholesale violations of the Red Cross principles on one side and protest reprisals against them . . .
>
> New York *Times* (International edition only), October 14, 1965

> Chances of surviving field interrogation are often extremely poor. Death can come for prisoners under the tracks of armored vehicles, by decapitation or by bleeding to death after both hands have been chopped off or by a bullet through the head. It's all part of the war in South Vietnam.
>
> Long Island *Newsday*, October 26, 1964

"I am, in fact, asking your Government—to quote your own Declaration of Independence—to display a decent respect for the opinions of mankind."

Michael Stewart, British Foreign Secretary, March 23, 1965

On October 21, 1965, the New York *Times* reported that Senator Stephen M. Young, who had just returned from a fact-finding mission to Vietnam, said:

> . . . that he had learned that the Central Intelligence Agency hired persons to disguise as Vietcong and discredit Communists in Vietnam by committing atrocities . . .
>
> Tonight, Senator Young . . . said that he got [the report] from an American military officer . . .
>
> "I confirmed through the C.I.A. today that it employed some South Vietnamese nationalists to pose as Vietcong—and I take a dim view of that," Mr. Young said.

Condolence payment in the equivalent of $33 was made to each of the families of seven children killed accidentally by an Air Force weapon. The money was in crisp new Vietnamese banknotes accompanied by a letter of "sympathy for the loss which you have suffered." *New York Times,* July 5, 1966.

In Congress it was reported that the cost of killing one guerrilla was $400,000.00

As the war escalates in intensity, the greatest sufferers are the civilians.

It is not only the Vietnamese who suffer.

War by its very nature is a cruel business. This war, however, differs from all others in which the United States has ever been engaged. In no previous conflict has the U.S. deployed so fearful a concentration of destructive power against so small a country. In the sheer mechanical brutality with which this war is being waged, it is unique. Never before has the young manhood of America been thrust into such a conflict or ordered to fight with methods that outrage both international law and the more general laws of our common humanity.

For this America's young men, as well as the Vietnamese, must pay a fearful price. All that is human, and generous in these young Americans can hardly survive the special horrors of this war. The corruption, the dehumanizing of the American boys in Vietnam may one day be seen as among the heaviest penalties of this war.

In July 1965 U.S. Marines fought a guerrilla force on the island of An Hoa

John T. Wheeler reported this engagement:

CIVILIANS, TOO. KILL THEM ALL, CHARGING MARINE SHOUTS.

> At the end of the village a woman lay gasping as blood poured from a wound in her side. Around her were clustered terrified children, wailing and alternately staring in fear at the Marines and turning to clutch the dying woman . . .
>
> The Marines burned down houses from which they believed the Viet Cong had fired . . .
>
> A Marine said several persons were burned seriously when one of the houses was touched off while its inhabitants were hiding in a bunker built into its floor.
>
> "Kill them, I don't want anyone moving," a marine said . . .
>
> New York *Herald Tribune* (Paris edition), August 3, 1965

How the Marines reacted to this "victory" was described by a U.P.I. dispatch:

> "I got me a VC, man. I got at least two of them bastards."
>
> The exultant cry followed a 10-second burst of automatic weapons fire yesterday, and the dull crump of a grenade exploding underground.
>
> The Marines ordered a Vietnamese corporal to go down into the grenade-blasted hole to pull out their victims.
>
> The victims were three children between 11 and 14—two boys and a girl. Their bodies were riddled with bullets . . .
>
> "Oh, my God," a young Marine exclaimed. "They're all kids." . . .
>
> Shortly before the Marines moved in, a helicopter had flown over the area warning the villagers to stay in their homes.
>
> New York *Herald Tribune,* August 3, 1965

Napalm is a highly inflammable jelly made by adding a chemical compound to aviation gasoline.

Charles Mohr reported (New York *Times,* September 5, 1965), what damage napalm can inflict on any one caught in its flames:

> In a delta province there is a woman who has both arms burned off by napalm and her eyelids so badly burned that she cannot close them. When it is time for her to sleep her family puts a blanket over her head. The woman had two of her children killed in the air strike . . . and she saw five other children die.

"For the first time since 1918, a democratic power is using gas and the outrage is, if anything, aggravated by the statement that these methods are being used on an 'experimental basis.' Thus the Americans, like Hitler and Mussolini in Spain, are treating the hapless inhabitants of Vietnam as a living laboratory in which to test their weapons."

New Statesman (London), March 26, 1965

Occasionally, through error, American troops have felt for themselves the effects of napalm bombing. A U.P.I. dispatch in the San Francisco *Chronicle* on November 17, 1965, describes such an incident:

> Suddenly I felt a searing heat on my face. An American fighter-bomber had misjudged the Communist positions, and dropped a load of napalm.
>
> The flaming jellied gasoline, impossible to shake or scrape off once it hits the skin, splashed along the ground in a huge dragon's tail of fire less than 25 yards away.

Screams pierced the roar of flames. Two Americans stumbled out of the inferno. Their hair burned off in an instant. Their clothes were incinerated. . . .

It was an hour before a medical helicopter could get into the area. . . . A medic asked me to help get the men into the helicopter when it arrived. There were no litters. Tenderly we picked the soldiers up. I held a leg of the most seriously burned man. I wasn't tender enough. A big patch of burned skin came off in my hand.

"The United States has now forfeited all right to British sympathy over Vietnam."

New Statesman (London), March 26, 1965

The *U.S. Chemical and Engineering News* has recently reported vastly increased procurement plans. In March 1966 the United Technology Center in Redwood City, California, got a contract for 100 million pounds of an "improved" napalm jelly. The magazine, as quoted in the London *New Statesman* of April 8, 1966, adds:

This is the Air Force's third procurement in the secrecy shrouded program in the past 18 months. . . . Predictions of future use of polystyrene in napalm-B now are running as high as 25 million pounds a month. . . . The U.S. combat forces in Vietnam are finding that the older formulations leave much to be desired, particularly in adhesion.

These last three words, comments the *New Statesman:*

. . . so glibly technical, refer to the capacity of this hateful substance to cling to the skin of the villagers on whom it is mainly dropped, so ensuring that they die in prolonged agony.

For the Vietnamese, to protest is dangerous. The Chicago *Daily News* (September 23, 1965) described how several people were publicly executed in Danang for taking part in a protest against crop damage from artillery fire and air attacks by U.S. forces. Dangerous, even, for the Vietnamese military. Colonel Pham Ngoc Thao (a former member of the ruling Government Advisory Council and a strong anti-Communist) wrote to *Newsweek* in Washington protesting that if the bombing policies of the U.S. Government continued, America would "lose the confidence of South Vietnam." Shortly afterwards a warrant was issued for Colonel Thao's arrest. The colonel went into hiding but was found by the secret police; the arresting officer shot him to death on the spot.

Pham Ngoc Thach, a Buddhist student leader, said to Neil Sheehan: "Look at the corpses on the battle field. The Vietcong are Communists but they are Vietnamese too. We are all the same people. We should not be killing each other like this."

New York *Times*, April 17, 1966

Stephen G. Cary of the Americans Friends Service Committee visited Vietnam to study the refugee situation there. On his return he reported:

The "no sanctuary" policy that is now being followed by United States . . . forces means that air support can be called instantly to destroy any village or hamlet from which sniper fire is reported or which is suspected of harboring Viet Cong troops. This policy is complemented by another which designates certain large enemy-held regions as "open target areas" where an aircraft unable to dispose of its explosives on the planned target may drop them at will on village, rice paddy, man or beast, wherever it suits the pilot's fancy.

"In the name of God, STOP IT!"

2,500 Ministers, Priests and Rabbis, in a letter to President Johnson

A U.S. official who had been first to enter a village after an American air strike told Cary:

> I could take everything but the dead kids. As a matter of fact I found only two persons alive—a boy of ten and his eight-year-old sister. They were sitting quietly on the ruins of their house, surrounded by the bodies of their mother and father and several other children.

Progressive, October 1965

If a Vietnamese peasant stays in his village he may die under U.S. fire; if he flees he may be shot by the advancing troops as an "escaping Viet Cong." Here is the fate of a Vietnamese farmer as described by Malcolm Browne in *The New Face of War* (pp. 5-6):

> Suddenly, a man leapt up about fifty yards away and began to run . . . Every machine gun, Tommy gun, rifle and pistol in our sector poured fire at that man, and I was amazed at how long he continued to run. But finally he went down, silently, without a scream . . .
>
> The group was detailed to go into the field to look for the man we had seen go down, and I went with them. We found him on his back in the mud, four bullet holes stitched across the top of his naked chest. He was wearing only black shorts. He was alive and conscious, moving his legs and arms, his head lolling back and forth. There was blood on his lips. The . . . squad . . . looked down at the man and laughed . . .
>
> Perhaps as an act of mercy, perhaps as sheer cruelty, one of the men picked up a heavy stake lying in the mud and rammed one end of it into the ground next to the wounded man's throat. Then he forced the stake down over the throat, trying to throttle the man. The man continued to move. Someone stamped on the free end of the stake to break the wounded man's neck, but the stake broke instead. Then another man tried stamping on the man's throat, but somehow the spark of life was still too strong. Finally, the whole group laughed, and walked back to the path. . . .
>
> . . . two women, both dressed in baggy black trousers and blouses, ran up from one of the huts. One of them put a hand to her mouth as she saw the wounded man, whom she recognized as her husband. She dashed back to her hut and returned in a moment carrying a bucket, which she carried with black water from the rice field. Sitting down with her husband's head cradled in her lap, she poured paddy water over his wounds to clean off the clotting blood. Occasionally she would stroke his forehead, muttering something. He died about ten minutes later. The woman remained seated, one hand over her husband's eyes. Slowly, she looked around at the troops, and then she spotted me. Her eyes fixed on me in an expression that still haunts me sometimes . . .

Americans! Americans! What has happened to you in Vietnam?

22. Ending

The war in Vietnam has been a moral disaster for the United States.

Many Americans, it appears, have been persuaded that there would be some thing shameful in withdrawing from Vietnam so as to allow the people there t settle their own affairs. Even those who have come to see that entering the wa was a huge and tragic blunder often add that "of course, we can't pull out now

But many others disagree.

> I, for one [wrote Henry W. Edgerton, Senior Circuit Judge of the United State Court of Appeals, in a letter to the New York *Times*], see no remaining reaso why our fighting men should not be brought home as fast as our ships and plan can carry them. If the President were to bring them home, instead of sending st more of them to kill and be killed in Vietnam and devastate the country, he . would gain the esteem of almost all humanity, including most of the people South Vietnam.

"Our commitment was to a 'legitimate government' and what we now have in Saigon is neither 'legitimate' nor a 'government'. . . . Our promise was to help South Vietnam, not to destroy it."

James Reston, New York *Times,* May 18, 1966

Prestige? What prestige, we must ask, will America retain if the war goes o as it is going now?

Was not the good name of France immeasurably enhanced, and in no wa diminished, when after years of bloody struggle she finally accepted what sh should have accepted years before, that Algeria belonged to the Algerians? An would not a similar acceptance by the United States in regard to Vietnam serv both her own national self-interest and also the cause of common humanity

The Vietnamese are a poor people. The average annual income of the peop of Vietnam is about $50 a year—what the average American earns in a sing week. The war today is costing the United States one million dollars *an hou* What could not the Vietnamese do for their country with what we spend in on day fighting them! It is costing the United States $400,000 to kill *one* guerrilla- enough to pay the annual income of 8,000 Vietnamese. What conceivable sens is there in a war of this kind? Is not the United States destined by its tradition its strength, and its material wealth for a nobler role in history than to fight on of the smallest and poorest countries in the world?

"Ah," say some, "we wish we could withdraw—but if we left, those who hav sided with us in Vietnam would all be slaughtered." We have heard this man times before. It was, for years, the standard pretext given by Great Britain fo not giving her colonies their independence; but when she withdrew the "slaugh ters" did not happen. "I think," said André Denis to the French Parliament 1950, "that withdrawal . . . would be more criminal than the war itself . . . th Vietnamese soldiers . . . would be exposed to a massacre . . . These people hav placed confidence in us." But when, after Dien Bien Phu, the French had n choice but to withdraw, there was no massacre.

No. We can no longer accept such a pretext. The massacre is now. The slaughter is now. To continue to burn women and children with napalm, to poison rice fields, to devastate a whole nation to save those who have sided with the destroyers is an excuse that can appeal only to the insane.

The United States cannot win this war. This, by now, should be clear.

> The harsh fact [said Major General Edward T. Lansdale], and one that has given pause to every thoughtful American, is that, despite the use of overwhelming amounts of men, money and *materiel,* despite the quantity of well-meant American advice . . . the Communist subversive insurgents have grown steadily stronger, in numbers and size of units. . . . The Communists have let loose a revolutionary idea in Vietnam and it will not die by being ignored, bombed or smothered by us. Ideas do not die in such ways.

That was written in October 1964; it hasn't changed much since.

The U.S. cannot win this war because it is for the first time directly confronting a war of liberation, a type of war whose politics and military techniques the United States' present culture simply cannot comprehend—though the United States itself began its national history with a war of liberation.

Not understanding the nature of this war, hopes for victory have been pinned first on this, then on that; but each new strategy, each new hope, has proved illusory. It was, at first, the Vietnamese with help from U.S. "advisers" that were going to accomplish it; then the helicopters; then the strategic hamlet plan; then the amphibious vehicles for flooded rice paddies; then the "Special Forces"; then defoliation; then napalm; then the bombing of north Vietnam; then the B-52's from Guam. And all the time the commitment grows, the huge vested interests that gain by the continuation of the war grow, the number of U.S. troops grows—and victory remains still somewhere beyond the horizon.

The United States can burn and devastate; it can annihilate the Vietnamese; but it cannot conquer them. And afterwards, if it annihilates them, and faces China across the smoking desert of Vietnam—what then?

The war itself has no legitimacy. The Vietnamese know it, the world knows it, and an increasing number of American citizens know it.

The United States cannot win this war because (in the only sense that matters) it has already lost it. For this country's honor has been lost. Even if it were possible, no military "victory," however complete, could restore lustre to the name of the United States. The people of the United States can regain the respect of the world only by making unmistakably clear by their voice and actions that this is not *their* war but only that of their political and military leaders. The day may yet come when the people of the United States will call their leaders to account for having so grossly misled them.

"[We] demand that ways be immediately found to disengage ourselves from this intolerable situation."

6,400 educators, artists, physicians, writers, scientists, and others in a letter to the government.

The people of the United States made their position clear at the last Presidential election—*they did not want this war*. In committing the country to the very military policy that the people then rejected, the Government of the United States not only betrayed its own people, but showed a lack of respect for the opinions of humane men everywhere.

Sooner or later the real meaning of the Vietnam war will be understood. The Vietnamese will remember it as an epic of almost unbelievable human fortitude. In the United States it will be recalled as a huge tragedy—perhaps the darkest hour of the nation's history. For it is one of the inescapable laws of life that no people can remain untouched by the tortures they inflict.

selected bibliography

Browne, Malcolm W. *The New Face of War*. New York: Bobbs-Merrill, 1965.

Burchett, Wilfred G. *Viet-Nam: Inside Story of the Guerrilla War*. New York: International Publishers, 1965.

Fall, Bernard B. *The Two Viet-Nams: A Political and Military History*. 5th rev. ed., New York: Praeger, 1965.

———. *Viet-Nam Witness*. New York: Praeger, 1966.

Gettleman, Marvin E. *Vietnam*. History, Documents, and Opinions on a Major World Crisis. Greenwich, Conn.: Fawcett, 1965.

Halberstam, David. *The Making of a Quagmire*. New York: Random House, 1965.

Lacouture, Jean. *Viet-Nam Between Two Truces*. New York: Random House, 1966.

Raskin, Marcus G., and Fall, Bernard B. *The Viet-Nam Reader*. Articles and Documents on American Foreign Policy and the Viet-Nam Crisis. New York: Random House (Vintage), 1965.

Scheer, Robert. *How the United States Got Involved in Vietnam*. Santa Barbara, Calif.: The Fund for the Republic, Inc., 1965.

Snow, Edgar. *War and Peace in Vietnam*. New York: Marzani and Munsell, 1965.

Warbey, M.P., William. *Vietnam: The Truth*. London: The Merlin Press, 1965.

AUTHOR'S NOTE:

I wish to draw special attention to Gettleman's *Vietnam* and to *The Viet-Nam Reader* by Raskin and Fall. These excellent books—both are paper-backs—are invaluable for anyone who needs to refer to the essential documents and articles regarding Vietnam. I made much use of them in preparing this book.

Another book to be highly recommended is Jean Lacouture's *Viet-Nam Between Two Truces*.

The American Friends Service Committee has issued two booklets, both of which are helpful: *Peace in Vietnam* and *The U.S. in Vietnam*.

I. F. Stone, in his admirable weekly, has given us a consistently high standard of reporting on Vietnam as on so many other important issues.

I am also greatly indebted to an article, "American Atrocities in Vietnam," by Eric Norden in the February 1966 issue of *Liberation*. I have, after checking the original sources, drawn freely from the many quotations Mr. Norden assembled for use in Section 21, "Prelude to Genocide." Mr. Norden's article should be read by everyone. Finally, no one wishing to grasp the full implications of U.S. policies in Vietnam can afford to ignore *Vietnam Primer*, issued by *Ramparts* magazine.

NOTE: Wherever italics have been used in quotations these have been added by the author unless a statement is made that the italics appeared in the original.

photo credits

Page		
Inside front cover		Wide World
2-3		Kyoichi Sawada, U.P.I.
8-9		E. Bourat, *Réalitiés*
10 to 13		D.R.V. Information Dept.
14 to 18		Acme
19	(top)	D.R.V. Information Dept.
	(bottom)	U.P.I.
20	(left)	U.P.I.
	(right)	Nicolas Tikhomiroff, Magnum
21	(top)	U.P.I.
	(bottom)	Acme
22 to 27		U.P.I.
28	(top)	U.P.I.
	(bottom)	PIX
29		U.P.I.
30		Wide World
32-33	(top left)	Wilfred Burchett, *National Guardian*
	(others)	D.R.V. Information Dept.
34	(left)	Wilfred Burchett, *National Guardian*
	(right)	D.R.V. Information Dept.
35	(top)	Wide World
	(bottom)	D.R.V. Information Dept.
36	(top)	D.R.V. Information Dept.
	(bottom)	U.P.I.
37		D.R.V. Information Dept.
38		Keystone
39		U.P.I.
40	(left)	U.P.I.
	(right)	Wide World
41		Akihiko Okamura, LIFE Magazine © Time, Inc.

Page		Credit
42		Kyoichi Sawada, U.P.I.
43 to 45		U.P.I.
46		Rene Burri, Magnum
48-49		Kyoichi Sawada, U.P.I.
50		U.P.I.
51		U.P.I.
52-53		Keystone
54		Martin Stuart-Fox, U.P.I.
55, 56		U.P.I.
57		Keystone
58-59		Keystone
60		U.P.I.
62-63		U.P.I.
64		Wide World
65		Wide World
66	(left)	U.P.I.
	(right)	Wide World
67		U.P.I.
68-69, 70		Wide World
71		Henry Huet, U.P.I.
72		Wide World
73	(left)	D.R.V. Information Dept.
	(right)	Wide World
74		U.P.I.
75		Joseph Galloway, U.P.I.
76-77		Keystone
78		U.P.I.
79		U.P.I.
80-81		Kyoichi Sawada, U.P.I.
82		U.P.I.
83	(top)	Bob Ibrahim, U.P.I.
	(bottom)	U.P.I.
84		Wide World
85, 86		Kyoichi Sawada, U.P.I.
87		U.P.I.
88-89		U.P.I.
90-91		U.P.I.
92		Wide World
93		U.P.I.
94 to 97		Felix Greene
98-99		U.P.I.
100, 101		Felix Greene
102, 103		D.R.V. Information Dept.
104 to 107		Felix Greene
108		Wide World
109		D.R.V. Information Dept.
110 to 113		Wide World
114-115		PIX
116-117		Wide World
118, 119		U.P.I.
Inside back cover		Wide World

index

P

R

S

T

U

V

W

Y

Z

FELIX GREENE was born and educated in Britain but has lived—off and on—more than half of his life in the United States. He was formely an official of the British Broadcasting Corporation and for some years headed the B.B.C. office in the United States.

Felix Greene is the only U.S.- based writer who has travelled to China on several occasions in recent years. His books "Awakened China" and "A Curtain of Ignorance" (both published by Doubleday) have received wide attention both here and abroad.

Felix Greene is known to lecture audiences throughout the United States. A film he photographed and produced "CHINA!" has also been shown in over one hundred U.S. cities after an initial run of twelve weeks at the Carnegie Hall Cinema in New York City. The film received the Award of Merit at the International Film Festival at Edinburgh, Scotland in 1965.

Felix Greene's most recent visit to the Far East was in the late fall of 1965. He spent five weeks in China before travelling on for a three-week visit to North Vietnam. He was the first western correspondent to have a filmed interview with President Ho Chi Minh, which was broadcast by the C.B.S. TV network, by the B.B.C. in Britain and in a large number of other countries.

For the past sixteen years Felix Greene has lived in Palo Alto, California.

Designed by Hubert Leckie

Production supervision Susan Lehmann

Printed by Double Dot Press, Washington, D.C.